Disney's

WONDERFUL WORLD OF KNOWLEDGE

YEAR BOOK 1985

Disney's

Wonderful
World of
Knowledge

YEAR BOOK 1985

GROLIER ENTERPRISES, INC.
Danbury, Connecticut

ROBERT B. CLARKE   *Publisher*

FERN L. MAMBERG   *Executive Editor*

MICHÈLE A. MCLEAN   *Art Director*

RICHARD SHAW   *Production Managers*
ALAN PHELPS

ISBN 0-7172-8148-5
The Library of Congress Catalog Card Number: 78-66149

CONTENTS

1984 AT A GLANCE

JANUARY 1. Brunei became an independent nation called Brunei Darussalam. The tiny country is located on the northern coast of the island of Borneo, in the Pacific Ocean. It had been under British protection for nearly 150 years. (In September, Brunei was admitted to the United Nations as its 159th member.)

FEBRUARY 7. Following a worsening of internal conditions in Lebanon, President Ronald Reagan ordered the U.S. Marines to withdraw from the country. The Marines were part of an international peacekeeping force that had been in Lebanon since the fall of 1982. (Later in February, Britain and Italy withdrew their troops. And in March the French, the last unit of the force, withdrew their troops. Thus ended the 19-month effort to keep peace in Lebanon.)

FEBRUARY 11. The space shuttle *Challenger* ended an eight-day mission by landing at Cape Canaveral, Florida. This was the first time that a shuttle had landed at its launching base. The five-man crew included Bruce McCandless and Robert Stewart, whose space walks were the highlight of the mission. The men used jet-propelled backpacks to move around in space. Unlike previous space walkers, they weren't connected to their ship by safety lines. They truly were "human satellites," orbiting Earth at the same speed as their spacecraft—17,500 miles per hour.

FEBRUARY 13. Konstantin U. Chernenko was chosen general secretary of the Soviet Communist Party's Central Committee. This is the most important position in the country. At the age of 72, he became the oldest person to lead the U.S.S.R. Chernenko succeeded Yuri V. Andropov, who had died earlier in the month.

FEBRUARY 29. Prime Minister Pierre Elliott Trudeau of Canada announced that he would resign as head of government and leader of the Liberal Party. Except for a nine-month period in 1979–1980, Trudeau had been prime minister since 1968. (On June 30, John N. Turner, the newly chosen head of the Liberal Party, became prime minister.)

MARCH 5. Lebanon canceled its 1983 troop withdrawal agreement with Israel. The U.S.-sponsored pact had called for the simultaneous withdrawal of Israeli, Palestine Liberation Organization (PLO), and Syrian troops from Lebanon. Syria had never accepted the agreement.

APRIL 3. Rakesh Sharma, a 35-year-old pilot, became India's first person in space. He and two Soviet astronauts were launched aboard a Soyuz T-11 spacecraft for an eight-day visit to the Salyut 7 earth-orbiting space station. During the mission, Sharma performed yoga exercises to test yoga's possible effectiveness in combating space sickness.

APRIL 13.   Astronauts aboard the U.S. space shuttle *Challenger* completed a seven-day mission. The mission's highlight was the first repair of a damaged satellite in space. The astronauts retrieved and repaired Solar Max, a satellite launched in 1980 to study the sun. The satellite had malfunctioned soon after its launch. After the repair work was completed, Solar Max was released back into orbit by the space shuttle's robot arm.

MAY 1.   U.S. President Ronald Reagan ended a six-day visit to China. During the trip he met with Chinese officials in an effort to strengthen ties between the two countries.

MAY 7.   The Soviet Union announced that it wouldn't participate in the 1984 Summer Olympic Games in Los Angeles. The Soviets claimed that the United States "does not intend to ensure the security of all sportsmen." (All the Warsaw Pact nations, except Rumania, eventually joined the boycott.)

MAY 23.   It was announced that archeologists had discovered an ancient Mayan tomb in the Petén jungle of northern Guatemala. The tomb was more than 1,500 years old and was in perfect condition. Its contents included wall paintings and pottery. Of special interest was a ceramic jar with a screw-top lid. Such a twist-open container had never before been found among remains of pre-Colombian cultures.

MAY 30. A nearly total solar eclipse could be seen in the southeastern United States. In most other parts of the United States and in Canada, a partial eclipse was visible. It was the last major solar eclipse to occur in North America during this century.

JUNE 1. A United Nations Security Council resolution condemned attacks on shipping in the Persian Gulf. The resolution was directed toward Iran, which had been accused by six Persian Gulf nations of carrying out such attacks. The attacks were part of the widening four-year-old war between Iran and Iraq.

JULY 19. At its national convention in San Francisco, the Democratic Party nominated Representative Geraldine A. Ferraro for vice-president. She was the first woman in U.S. history to be the vice-presidential candidate of a major party.

JULY 25. A Soviet astronaut, Svetlana Savitskaya, became the first woman to walk in space. Savitskaya spent more than three hours outside the Salyut 7 space station.

AUGUST 4. The West African country of Upper Volta changed its name to Burkina Faso. The name change marked the first anniversary of a coup that had set up the current military government.

SEPTEMBER 4. In national elections in Canada, the Progressive Conservative Party won 211 of the 282 seats in parliament—the most seats won by any party in Canadian history. The party's leader, Brian Mulroney, thus became prime minister, effective September 17. He succeeded John Turner of the Liberal Party, who had been prime minister for 79 days.

SEPTEMBER 5. The U.S. space shuttle *Discovery* completed its maiden flight. The six-member crew spent six days in space.

SEPTEMBER 15. Diana, Princess of Wales, gave birth to her second son, who was named Prince Henry. The baby is third in line for the British crown after his father, Prince Charles, and his brother, Prince William.

SEPTEMBER 25. Jordan announced that it was restoring diplomatic relations with Egypt. Jordan was one of seventeen Arab nations that had broken diplomatic relations with Egypt in 1979, after Egypt had signed a peace treaty with Israel. It became the first of these nations to resume diplomatic ties.

OCTOBER 2. Three Soviet astronauts returned to Earth after spending 237 days in space—setting a new space-endurance record. They had been sent aloft in a Soyuz spacecraft in February, to perform various experiments aboard the Salyut 7 space station.

OCTOBER 13. The U.S. space shuttle *Challenger* completed an eight-day mission. The seven-member crew included two women and Canada's first astronaut, Marc Garneau. Kathryn D. Sullivan became the first American woman to walk in space.

OCTOBER 31. India's Prime Minister Indira Gandhi, 66, was assassinated by two gunmen who were members of her bodyguard. Her son, Rajiv, was chosen as her successor, thereby continuing a political dynasty that began with his grandfather Jawaharlal Nehru. Nehru was prime minister during India's first seventeen years of independence from Britain. Indira Gandhi served as her father's official hostess and close political ally. Following his death in 1964, she was elected to parliament and in 1966 became prime minister. Except for three years (1977–1980), she held the position until her death.

NOVEMBER 6. In U.S. elections, Republicans Ronald W. Reagan and George H. Bush were re-elected president and vice-president. They defeated Democratic candidates Walter F. Mondale and Geraldine A. Ferraro.

NOVEMBER 16. Astronauts aboard the space shuttle *Discovery* completed an eight-day mission. The five-member crew retrieved two communications satellites that had misfired into useless orbits after their launch in February. The satellites were brought back to Earth in *Discovery*'s cargo bay.

DECEMBER 4. Scientists announced the discovery and excavation of a ship that sank off the southern coast of Turkey about 3,400 years ago. It was the earliest shipwreck ever excavated. The ship was a treasure trove of Bronze Age artifacts, including gold objects, beads, pottery, and copper and tin ingots.

ABC'S OF BODY TALK

A frog in your throat . . . butterflies in your stomach . . . goose bumps on your arms . . . sand in your eyes. What is your body saying?

Your body constantly reacts, or talks back, to the world in which it lives. It talks back to germs that try to invade it. It talks back to embarrassing stories, to chilly weather, to sleepless nights.

Which of the following are part of your body talk?

Black and Blue Marks. Sometimes you bang a part of your body against a hard object. Your skin doesn't break. But there's damage, and your skin turns "black and blue." What happened? When you bump yourself, small blood vessels just under the skin's surface are broken, and blood seeps out of the vessels. Your body stops this bleeding in the same way that it stops bleeding from a cut—the blood thickens and forms a clot. Blood that clots under the skin appears a dark purple. As fluids in your body break down the clot, the color changes to blue, then green, then yellow. Finally, the black and blue mark disappears.

Blushing. Someone embarrasses you—and your face turns bright pink. Why? When you are embarrassed, you get excited. Your brain tells your heart to pump faster. It also tells the capillaries (tiny blood vessels) in your body to get wider, so they can carry the extra blood being pumped out of the heart. You usually don't notice the extra blood that rushes to your arms or legs. But you do notice it in your face. And so does everyone else—the rushing blood makes the skin of your face flush with color.

Burps. Burps are your body's way of releasing air you have swallowed. As you eat and drink, you swallow air. You also swallow air that is trapped in food and drinks, such as in sodas. As more and more air fills your stomach, more and more pressure builds up. When there is enough pressure, the air pushes its way up and out. It goes up through the esophagus (the tube that leads from your stomach to your mouth). When it reaches the top of the esophagus, it rushes out with a funny noise—a burp.

Butterflies in Your Stomach. Your stomach is constantly moving, churning the food you've eaten and pushing it slowly toward the small intestine. If you are upset about something, your brain may tell your stomach muscles to stop working in order to save energy. It does this so that other muscles in your body will have enough energy to deal with whatever is upsetting you. When the smooth movement of the stomach is suddenly disrupted, it feels as if a bunch of butterflies were doing flip flops inside you.

Circles Under Your Eyes. The skin below your eyes is very thin and filled with hundreds of tiny blood vessels. Usually, the blood in these vessels is rich in oxygen and red in color. But when you're very tired or when you don't sleep well, your blood doesn't circulate at its usual speed. Old blood, low in oxygen and bluish in color, collects in the vessels, forming dark rings below your eyes.

Frog in Your Throat. Sometimes your vocal cords may be sore, either from using your voice too much or from an infection. When this happens, you sound hoarse, or as though

you have a "frog" in your throat. As soon as your vocal cords heal, the frog disappears.

Goose Bumps. Almost every part of your body is covered with tiny, often invisible hairs. At the base of most hairs is a tiny muscle. When your skin gets cold, these muscles tighten in an effort to help stop the loss of heat. This makes the hairs stand up, forming little bumps. You can also get goose bumps when you're under stress or frightened. When you get nervous, glands in your body may secrete a chemical called adrenaline. Adrenaline helps your body deal with emergencies. Among other things, adrenaline tightens the tiny hair muscles, causing goose bumps.

Hiccups. Hiccups can be annoying. They seem to start up for no reason, and they can be hard to stop. Hiccups occur when something goes wrong with your diaphragm (a flat, sheetlike muscle between your chest and abdomen that helps you breathe). Usually the diaphragm contracts and expands smoothly and regularly, and breathing is normal. But sometimes, and no one is quite sure why, the diaphragm becomes irritated and starts to make abrupt little contractions, or

15

Sand in Your Eyes. Tears are a fluid that contains salt and other chemicals. This fluid is constantly secreted by glands behind your eyelids. At night when you are asleep, the tears collect in the corners of your eyes. Gradually the fluid dries out, leaving behind the chemicals. These form the crusty, sticky "sand" that you rub from your eyes when you awaken in the morning.

Shriveled Skin. If you spend too much time relaxing in a hot bath, your hands and feet may look like wrinkled prunes. This doesn't happen to the skin on other parts of your body because that skin contains sebaceous glands. These glands secrete an oily substance that coats the skin and lessens the amount of water leaving the body. But the skin on your hands and feet doesn't contain sebaceous glands. Thus water inside your skin slowly oozes out into the bathwater. Your skin is actually drying from the inside out. If your skin loses too much water, some of its cells collapse, causing the skin to shrivel.

Snoring. If you breathe through your mouth when you sleep, you may be snoring. As air rushes in and out of your mouth, the soft palate (soft tissue in the roof of the mouth

jerks. This disrupts the smooth intake of air into the lungs and produces a noise that sounds like "hiccup." Hiccups are most likely to happen when you eat or drink too quickly, when someone tickles you, or when you laugh a lot.

Lump in Your Throat. You worry about something, and the muscles in your body tighten. Even the muscles in your throat may tense up. And this is what makes you feel as if you have a "lump" in your throat and can't swallow. The problem quickly disappears when you calm down.

Mouth Watering. You smell cookies baking, or you think about your favorite pizza. Your brain automatically remembers that cookies and pizza are foods you like to eat. So it prepares your body for eating by telling glands near your mouth to start giving off saliva—thus making your mouth water. (Saliva is a fluid that moistens food and makes it easier to swallow. It also contains chemicals that help digest food.)

near the throat) vibrates. This vibration produces the rough, sawing sound of snoring. Nearly everyone snores sometimes. But you'll be most likely to snore if your nose is stuffed up from a cold or if you sleep on your back.

Spots Before Your Eyes. If someone takes your picture with a flashbulb, you may see spots for a few seconds after the flash goes off. Why? When light enters your eyes, it hits the cells in the retina (the thin inner coat of the eyeball). Chemical changes occur in these cells, and this causes messages to be sent to the brain about what you are seeing. But if you look at a very bright light, such as a camera flashbulb, you expose the cells to too much light. The overexposed cells create the spots before your eyes.

Sweat. You're playing tennis on a hot summer day, and you're drenched in perspiration. What's happening? Your body is sweating to help you cool off. Sweat is a salty liquid that is produced by glands in the skin. It moves through the narrow glands to openings, or pores, in the surface of the skin. The sweat spreads over the warm skin. As it evaporates, it takes heat away from the skin. On a hot day, an adult will sweat about a quart (.9 liter) of liquid.

Tears. Do you think of tears as something your eyes produce when you are sad? Actually, you have tears in your eyes 24 hours a day. Tears are a fluid containing salts and other chemicals. They are constantly secreted by glands behind the eyelids, and they moisten and protect the eyes. If a speck of dirt, for example, gets in your eyes, tears wash it away. But when you're very unhappy, the muscles around the tear glands tighten. This squeezes a great deal of fluid out of the glands. The fluid collects in your eyes until there is so much of it that the tears run down your face. The same thing may happen when you laugh very hard.

Tickle in Your Throat. A thick, sticky substance called mucus keeps your throat moist. But if you breathe in dust or if the air is very dry, part of your throat may dry out. This creates an irritation, or a "tickle." You usually react by coughing. If that doesn't work, a drink of water should do the trick.

Yawning. When you're tired, or bored, or even just very relaxed, your body ceases to

be alert. Your breathing and heartbeat slow down. As a result, there's less oxygen in your bloodstream. Your brain reacts by forcing a yawn. Yawning opens up the air sacs in your lungs, so that more oxygen can enter the blood. But scientists can't explain everything about yawning. For instance, they don't know why yawning is contagious—why people sometimes yawn just because they see someone else yawning. And do you *pandiculate* when you yawn? In plainer English, this asks if you stretch your arms when you yawn. Lots of people do!

JENNY TESAR
Series Consultant, *Wonders of Wildlife*

The chameleon, a lizard whose name means "little lion," is best known for its ability to change colors.

QUICK-CHANGE ARTISTS

A small brown chameleon sits on a shady branch. Only an alert observer would spot it. Later, that same chameleon moves through sunlit leaves. Within seconds its skin turns a bright green. Once again it blends into its environment, becoming invisible to its enemies and to the insects it hopes to catch.

The chameleon's ability to change color is probably its best-known feature. But contrary to what many people believe, a chameleon doesn't change color just to match its surroundings. More often, changes occur in response to temperature, light, and the animal's mood. In the warm, bright light of day, chameleons generally display vivid colors. At night, when it's comparatively cool, they fade to a pale color. If a chameleon is frightened, it will change colors, becoming very noticeable. It will turn pale when it is ill. And a female chameleon may become brightly colored just before she begins to lay eggs.

The colors a chameleon can change into vary from species to species. Generally they include shades of yellow, green, and brown. Blues, reds, and black may also be present. The color may be uniform over the chameleon's body. Or there may be colored patterns of spots or stripes.

Chameleons are able to change their body color because of special color cells, called chromatophores, in their skin. These cells contain all the color pigments that an individual chameleon has. One of these pigments is melanin, a dark-colored substance that moves around the cells and plays a major role in the lizard's color changes. As a chameleon responds to a situation, nerve impulses are sent to the chromatophores. And the melanin there moves according to the commands sent by the impulses. For example, if a chameleon moves among bright green leaves, the melanin contracts into a small area of each cell, allowing the green pigment to dominate. When the animal moves onto a dark branch, the melanin spreads throughout each cell, masking the green and other bright pigments.

"LITTLE LIONS"

There are about 90 species of chameleons. They belong to the lizard family *Chamaeleontidae*. Most live in southern Africa or Madagascar, but a few can be found along the Mediterranean and in Asia. None are natives of the Americas—although many people incorrectly call the American anole lizard a chameleon.

Chameleons have massive heads and flat, scaly bodies. Their bulging eyes are almost completely covered by scaly lids. Some species have horns on the head, and many have a crest along the back or under the throat. Most chameleons grow to about a foot (30 centimeters) in length. But some pigmy chameleons are only 2 inches (5 centimeters) long, and the largest chameleons measure nearly 2 feet (60 centimeters) from snout to tail.

Although some species of chameleons make their homes on the ground, most live in trees and bushes. They are amazingly well-adapted to life in the trees. They have feet that grip like hands, and they are the only lizards that have gripping tails. Chameleons are so perfectly suited to tree life that they rarely venture down. Usually they do so only to move to another tree or to bury eggs—the females of some species dig nests in the ground for the eggs they lay. (Other species give birth to live young.)

Looking like a harmless leaf or part of a branch, a chameleon spends most of its time just lying in wait for prey. Chameleons are extremely good hunters. In fact, they have been named for their hunting skills: The word "chameleon" comes from a Greek word meaning "little lion." In addition to using color changes, the chameleon has two other adaptations that aid in hunting—its eyes and its tongue.

A chameleon's large, bulging eyes can look in two directions at once. One eye can look forward while the other swivels around to see what's behind. This means that the lizard can check out the entire neighborhood without moving and without giving itself away. But once an insect comes into view, the chameleon focuses both eyes on it. Slowly the chameleon creeps toward the prey. Once in range, it is ready to use its special weapon—its tongue.

Fully extended, a chameleon's tongue may be longer than its body, and it can be shot forward with lightning speed. The tip is covered with a sticky substance that catches and holds its prey. Powerful muscles controlling the tongue draw it back with the fresh meal attached. The prehistoric-looking little lizard will then quietly lie in wait until another unsuspecting victim comes along!

When a hungry chameleon wants to dine, it catches the prey with a special weapon—its tongue.

Home computers are useful in an amazing number of ways. And with special hardware called peripherals, your computer can do even more tasks. For example, with a printer attached, you can use your computer for school reports and homework.

MY COMPUTER: WHAT CAN I DO WITH IT?

• Mark is planning a trip to Puerto Rico. He uses his home computer to make airplane and hotel reservations . . . and to buy vacation clothes.

• Suzanne uses her computer to learn how to type. First she learned the correct positions for her fingers. Now she is playing a computer game in which giant words fall from the sky. They can be repelled only by typing the same words on the computer keyboard. The better Suzanne types, the faster the words fall and the more exciting the game is.

• Diane covers high school sports for a local newspaper. She writes her articles on a computer. A special attachment that connects the computer to a telephone lets Diane send each article directly from her home to the newspaper.

• Steve has designed a computer game and wants to sell it to other computer owners. He places an ad on an electronic bulletin board and then uses his computer to call the bulletin board for messages.

Millions of people are crazy about their home computers. Why? Because the machines are useful in such an amazing number of ways. They provide fun and entertainment in the form of computer games. And they make a variety of jobs—from writing a report for school to managing a business—easier and more efficient.

To get a computer to do what you want it to do, you must give it a set of instructions. The instructions are called a program, or *software*. (The computer and any machines attached to it are called *hardware*.) You can write software yourself, or you can buy software that has been written by other people. Thousands of commercial software programs are available, and the number increases every day.

For some tasks, you need special hardware called *peripherals*. For example, if you want to use your computer to write letters or school reports, you need a printer attached to the computer. If you want the computer to "talk" with a computer in a distant town, you need to use a *modem*. This device connects the computer to your telephone line.

Your Private Tutor. A computer is an excellent learning tool. People like to learn with computers because they can learn at their own speed. There is also constant interaction between the person and the computer. The computer immediately tells if an answer is correct. And if an answer is wrong, the computer doesn't get angry or make the person feel stupid.

There are educational programs for people of all ages, from preschoolers to adults. Some programs are tutorials—they teach specific subjects such as algebra or computer programming. Others provide drill and practice (the typing game played by Suzanne is an example). Still other educational programs are simulations. That is, they imitate the way things happen in real life. One popular simulation asks you to operate a nuclear power plant. You must try to supply electricity profitably. Otherwise, you'll lose your license to operate the plant.

The Expert Writer. When you write letters or reports, are they filled with erasures and misspellings? Do you often have to rewrite something because you forgot to include information or because you need to make changes? A home computer with a printer and word processing software will help solve these problems. Writing letters, term papers, or even a novel is faster and easier on a computer than by hand.

Let's say that you want to write a letter. As you type on the computer keyboard, the text appears on the screen. If you want to make a change, you move a special flashing mark (the *cursor*) to the place in the text where the change is desired. Press a few keys—and the text is just the way you want it. When you have finished the letter, you can use a spelling checker program. This will point out any spelling errors you may have made and give you the chance to correct them. When the letter is finished, press a few more keys and it will be printed onto paper, with no typographical errors.

Shape Up. Software products designed to help people become healthier are now quite popular. These include nutrition, exercise, and biofeedback programs.

Some nutrition programs keep track of what you eat. This lets you make sure that

Many educational programs for young people teach specific subjects, such as reading and writing.

BULLETIN BOARD

1 Graffiti
2 Listening Post
3 Art Gallery
4 Neighborhood Chat
5 Ask The Expert
6 You're The Expert
7 Viewpoint
8 Nat'l Bulletin Board

NOTICE
View Back-to-School Art Contest winners in Art Gallery.

0 MESSAGES INDEX

If you have a modem you can use your computer to hook up to "bulletin boards," which allow you to exchange messages with other computer owners. The computer screen shown above is a bulletin board index. Choosing one option—for example, Ask the Expert—leads to a list of fourteen bulletin boards *(below).* In each. you can ask questions of an expert in that subject. And the expert will answer you via his or her computer.

ASK THE EXPERT

HAVE QUESTIONS? OUR EXPERTS ARE STANDING BY WITH HELPFUL ADVICE. LOOK FOR THIS SYMBOL.

1 CARPET MART
2 CITY HALL
3 CONSUMER ISSUES
4 CRIME WATCH
5 DON'S GOLF
6 FASHION & BEAUTY
7 HOUSEHOLD HINTS
8 NUTRITION
9 PERSONAL ADVICE
10 PET CARE
11 PLANT CARE
12 PUBLIC LIBRARY
13 RELIGION
14 TRAVEL

0 BULLETIN BOARD INDEX

you are getting the right amounts of vitamins, proteins, and other nutrients. Other programs help you plan well-balanced meals that are within your budget. One software package provides information on food additives and gives advice on how to improve your eating habits.

There is software that helps you plan personalized exercise programs based on your fitness level. Other software shows you how to do aerobic exercises and keeps track of your progress.

Biofeedback programs train you to relax. When you aren't relaxed, your muscles are tense and the electrical resistance in your skin is comparatively high. By attaching a monitor to your body and connecting it to the computer, you can measure muscle tension or electrical resistance and see how it changes as you do various relaxation exercises. The computer screen usually shows this information in the form of a graph.

Running a Business. Running a business can be very complicated and time-consuming. But software programs can make many business-related chores easier. For example, let's say that you have a small business making fancy salads. You sell the salads to neighbors and to people at school. You can use your computer to keep a list of customers, their addresses, what salads they like, how often they have ordered from you, and how much money they owe. If you want to send the customers an advertisement, you can write the ad on the computer and then print as many copies as you need. You can also ask the computer to use the customer list to produce mailing labels for the ad.

You'll want to keep track of your business expenses and income. This information can be kept in an accounting program. Each time you take in or spend money, type the information into the computer. The computer immediately recalculates all the information you have given it so that it can provide an up-to-the-minute picture of how your business is doing.

Information, Please. If you have a modem, you can use your computer to obtain information from data banks. A data bank is like a library—it is a collection of information (data). Different data banks contain different types of information. For example, a stock market data bank contains current information on stock prices. An airline reservation data bank contains information on flight times, ticket costs, and seating options.

Some computer data banks are interactive. Instead of simply reading what they contain, you can add your own information. For example, an airline data bank may let you type in reservations for a trip you plan to take.

Several companies, known as *information utilities,* provide access to many data banks.

You pay a fee to hook up to a utility. When you call the utility, you indicate what information you want. This could be a weather report, today's baseball scores, an encyclopedia article on space missions, or reviews of a new movie.

Information utilities usually provide another service: electronic bulletin boards. These are used for exchanging messages with other computer owners. To use one, you turn on your computer and dial the bulletin board. When the phone answers, your computer automatically connects to the bulletin board computer. You can type in messages for other people or ask to see messages that were left for you.

Shopping and Banking at Home. Companies are beginning to offer consumers computer shopping services. Information about items for sale is shown on the screen. If you want to order an item, you simply press certain keys on the computer. The object is mailed to you, and its cost is billed to your credit card account. In some places, it's even possible to use a home computer to do grocery shopping. You enter your order via the modem, and later in the day the store has someone deliver your groceries.

Several dozen experimental banking programs are now underway. They let you use your computer to do simple banking transactions: check account balances, transfer money from one account to another (within the same bank), get an instant record of recent transactions, and pay bills.

Computerized Files. Specialized software makes it easy for people to store various information in computerized files. There are genealogical programs for people who gather data on their ancestors. There are programs that let you keep an inventory of all your personal belongings.

Perhaps you have a record collection. Which records contain Song A? Which are performed by Singer X? It's relatively easy to set up a computer file on a collection. The file can contain almost any kind of information you wish, it's easy to keep up to date, and it takes up much less space than a paper file.

Let's Play! Entertainment—having fun—is one of the main uses of home computers. There are many types of computer games.

Some are target-shooting games that require co-ordination and split-second timing. Others, such as chess, require an ability to plan ahead. Mystery stories and adventure games involve reasoning—you are given information that you must use to find the solution.

Some software can be used for both entertainment and work. Graphics programs let you create pictures on the screen. You can draw computer pictures for pleasure. Or you can create charts and graphs for school projects or business purposes. You can have your computer save the pictures so that they can be looked at over and over again, or you can have the computer print the pictures on paper.

And Many More . . . Look through a computer magazine or visit a store that sells software. A quick glance will show you that there are many additional uses to which you can put your home computer. You may see a program that allows you to control a home security system. You may see one that will turn electrical appliances on and off. You may see a peripheral that gathers weather information and feeds it into your computer so that the computer can predict how warmly you should dress if you're going outdoors. What other software is available? Go and see!

JENNY TESAR
Designer, Computer Programs

THE GREAT CHOCOLATE BINGE

Thick, glossy chocolate bars studded with almonds . . . chocolate-coated candies oozing creamy fillings . . . fresh strawberries dipped by hand in tubs of melted chocolate . . . chocolate ice cream, chocolate-chip cookies, chocolate syrup in your milk.

Has the world gone on a chocolate binge? So it seems. In the United States, people are eating more chocolate than ever—on the average, more than 9 pounds (4 kilograms) a year for every man, woman, and child in the country. Europeans eat still more chocolate. The average Belgian, for example, eats 15 pounds (7 kilograms) a year.

Why are people going crazy over chocolate? For the most part, they simply love the taste. But chocolate has also become high fashion. People are paying more than $30 a pound for gourmet chocolates that carry a famous name. Exclusive shops in some cities carry fresh chocolates that are flown in daily from Europe. Others specialize in custom chocolate designs—one such firm will reproduce your portrait in chocolate.

Buttons and T-shirts proclaim the love of chocolate. Resorts hold special chocolate-binge weekends. There are all-chocolate cookbooks. There's even a bimonthly newsletter called *Chocolate News*—which is printed on chocolate-scented paper and brings its readers the latest word on such items as chocolate chili and chocolate dog biscuits. And *Chocolate: The Consuming Passion,* a recent book that pokes fun at the craze, has sold thousands of copies.

THE "FOOD OF THE GODS"

Chocolate has always been considered something of an exclusive treat. In the 1500's, Spanish explorers in South America found Indians drinking a dark liquid made from the beans of the cacao tree. They took some beans back to Spain and added sugar to the drink. For years, chocolate was a secret closely kept by the Spanish nobility. But eventually word of the delicious substance got out. In 1775, the Swedish botanist Carolus Linnaeus gave the cacao tree its scientific name—*Theobroma,* from Greek words meaning "food of the gods." Today most of the world's cacao is grown in West Africa, although South America still grows a substantial amount.

Turning beans into chocolate is a complicated process. It takes about 400 beans to make a pound of chocolate. The beans are first fermented, dried, sorted, and roasted. Then they are shelled, and the soft centers are crushed to form the dark liquid known as chocolate liquor. (Despite its name, it contains no alcohol.) More than 50 percent of the chocolate liquor is made up of fat, called cocoa butter.

Hardened chocolate liquor is sold as unsweetened baking chocolate. To make powdered cocoa, most of the fatty cocoa butter is pressed out of the liquor, and what's left is ground and sifted. To make chocolate candy, extra cocoa butter, sugar, vanilla, and sometimes milk are added to the chocolate liquor. The mixture is placed in a huge tub, where it is blended and smoothed for anywhere from a few hours to several days. Then it is heated to remove fat crystals and molded into its final form. But chocolate makers won't tell the details of their recipes and processes. They consider chocolate making an art.

CHOCOLATE AND HEALTH

Chocolate lovers say that the flavor of their favorite treat just can't be duplicated artificially. And they may be right—chocolate consists of more than 300 chemical substances. But while millions of people are bingeing on chocolate, what's happening to their health? Are some of those substances harmful?

Chocolate has been blamed for helping to cause acne, tooth decay, obesity, and heart disease. Nutritionists agree that chocolate is certainly not a health food. It's high in fat and sugar. That means it's high in calories, so while chocolate is a good source of energy, it can also make you put on weight. But, the nutritionists say, chocolate is no worse than any other sweet. In fact, if you must eat candy, chocolate may be a good choice. It contains small amounts of protein, calcium, and iron, which your body needs.

Cocoa, chocolate syrup, and instant chocolate powders are the most healthful forms of chocolate because they contain the least fat. Two tablespoons of instant powder have about 55 calories. Chocolate candy has much more fat. A typical chocolate bar has 220 calories. But chocolate doesn't contain cholesterol, a fatty substance that's thought to cause heart disease.

A few people are allergic to chocolate—they may get headaches or break out in rashes. But studies have shown that for most people, chocolate doesn't cause acne.

Chocolate does contain small amounts of caffeine, a stimulant. Too much caffeine can make you nervous and keep you awake at night, and it can also harm your health. But chocolate has only about 10 percent of the caffeine found in coffee. Chocolate has larger amounts of another stimulant, theobromine. But because theobromine acts on muscles rather than nerves, it won't make you nervous or keep you awake.

Another chemical in chocolate is phenylethylamine. This chemical is produced naturally in the brain, especially when people are feeling loved and loving. Some doctors have suggested that unhappy people may crave chocolate because they're not producing any phenylethylamine of their own.

What about tooth decay? Rather than causing cavities, some researchers think, chocolate may actually help prevent them. One study found that people who ate a pound of chocolate a week had no more cavities than people who ate no sweets. People who ate other kinds of candy, though, had five times as many cavities.

Of course, any sweet is bad for you if you eat too much of it. The fat and sugar in chocolate can fill you up quickly. Then you won't be hungry for more nutritious foods. But if you're not overweight and you know you're getting all the nutrients your body needs, you can give in to your chocolate craving every now and then. Enjoy!

For a real sweet treat, make an old-fashioned soda fountain drink — a chocolate egg cream: Fill a glass half with club soda and half with milk. Add several tablespoons of chocolate syrup and stir until frothy.

LARGER THAN LIFE

What can travel a mile in a hop, a step, and a jump? Carry a coach-and-four slung over one shoulder? Uproot a tree as if it were a blade of grass?

A giant, of course. From ancient times to the present, stories and legends have told of these marvelous mythical creatures—like humans but vastly larger and stronger. Some have been portrayed as evil monsters, plundering the countryside and devouring human flesh. Others have been described as helpful and kindly, although perhaps a bit clumsy. And all kinds of wonderful feats are said to have been accomplished by giants. According to some stories, giants even shaped the landscape of the earth.

GIANTS IN ANCIENT MYTH

Legends from many parts of the world tell of giants who roamed the earth before people appeared. Some Indian tribes, for example, believed that giant Indians once lived in North America. They were tall enough to carry buffalo over their shoulders. Some Norse myths tell that the world was created from the body of a terrible giant, Ymir, who was killed by the gods. From his flesh they made the soil; from his blood, the seas; from his bones, the mountains; from his hair, the trees; from his skull, the sky. The gods then walled off the world of humans with Ymir's eyelashes, to protect it from other giants.

The ancient Greeks also believed that gigantic creatures lived long before the first people were born. These giants were the children of the Earth (Gaea) and the Sky (Uranus). Three of them were enormously huge and strong, with a hundred arms and fifty heads each. Three others were cyclops—they had just one eye each, right in the middle of the forehead. The rest were the Titans, just as huge and strong but not quite as evil as the others. According to legend, a Titan named Cronus rebelled against Uranus and wounded him.

Cronus ruled the universe for ages, until his son, the god Zeus, revolted. In the war between the Titans and the gods, the Titans were defeated. The Titans were eventually banished beneath the surface of the earth. But according to other legends, there were still some cyclops roaming about.

The most famous of these was Polyphemus. On his way home from the Trojan War, the Greek hero Odysseus led his men unawares into Polyphemus' cave. Before long, the giant came home, herding his sheep into the cave and rolling a huge stone across the entrance to block it. The men were trapped. And when Polyphemus saw them, he started to make them his dinner. But Odysseus tricked the giant. First, he gave him strong wine to drink. When the giant fell asleep, Odysseus and his men put out his single eye. Enraged, the blinded giant opened the cave and waited with his hands outstretched to catch the men as they ran out. But Odysseus had tied each of his men to the belly of a sheep, so the giant felt only sheep go by.

Michèle

THE GIANTS OF BRITAIN

A race of giants was said to have lived in England in early times, too. People believed that these giants built Stonehenge, a prehistoric ring of towering rocks in southern England, and set up similar stones elsewhere. The giants were supposed to be the children of 33 evil daughters of the Roman emperor Diocletian, each of whom had murdered her husband. The daughters were set adrift in a boat and arrived in England, where they married demons and gave birth to the giants.

The giants were the only inhabitants of England for many years. Then, the stories tell, the hero Brut—who was also returning from the Trojan war—arrived to fight them. He dug a huge trench and hid it with branches, so that when the giants charged in battle they fell in. Those who weren't killed were driven to Cornwall, in the far southwest. But the two most powerful giants, Gog and Magog, were taken prisoner. They were chained to the gates of Brut's palace in London and made to serve as porters. Today statues of Gog and Magog guard the doors of the London Guildhall, which is said to stand on the site of Brut's palace.

If folk tales can be believed, though, there were still plenty of giants around—especially in Cornwall. One of the best known of

these tales concerns a Cornish boy named Jack, who lived at the time of King Arthur. He set out to rid his neighborhood of a dreadful pest—the giant Cormoran.

Cormoran was 18 feet tall and 9 feet around. He was a fearsome monster who raided the countryside, carrying off half a dozen oxen and three times that many sheep and hogs at a time. But Jack killed him with the same trick Brut had used: a concealed pit. From there Jack went on to kill five more giants—or perhaps many more, depending on the version of the story you read. He became known far and wide as Jack the Giant-Killer.

Not all the British giants were pests like Cormoran. The giant of Grabbist, in Somerset, was a helpful soul. He even waded into the sea to save small boats that were foundering in storms.

A LAND OF GIANTS

Can you picture a country in which everything—from flies to fields of wheat—is scaled to giant size? Such a land was described by the British writer Jonathan Swift in *Gulliver's Travels*, which was published in 1726.

In the story, Gulliver's ship is blown off course and stops to pick up water along a strange coast. By accident, Gulliver is left

behind. He soon finds himself walking through a field of grain—grain that is 40 feet high! Before long he is captured by a farmer, who "appeared as tall as an ordinary spire-steeple and took about ten yards at every stride." Gulliver is a great curiosity to the farmer and his family, and the farmer begins to carry him from town to town to show him off. Eventually he is bought by the queen of the country. He is kept in a little carrying box that to him is the size of a room, and he becomes the pet of the royal family.

In this strange country, which is called Brobdingnag, flies are the size of songbirds. Songbirds are the size of swans. Horses are 60 feet tall. The giants' voices sound like thunder. And Gulliver nearly loses his life when he is picked up and cuddled by a giant-size monkey.

Gulliver finally escapes from Brobdingnag when his "room" is carried off by an enormous eagle and dropped in the ocean. In another part of the book, he visits Lilliput. There the people are just 6 inches high. To them, Gulliver is a giant!

GIANTS IN AMERICA

Britain isn't the only country that has tales of giants, of course. There are stories from all over the world. A German tale tells of a young man who must fetch three golden hairs from the head of a giant in order to win the hand of a princess. There are Danish stories about a ghostly giant who haunts a forest called the Grunewald. And nearly every country has its own version of Jack and the Beanstalk, in which a boy climbs up a magic stalk to steal the treasures of a giant.

American folklore has its own giants. One of the most famous is Paul Bunyan, the legendary lumberjack.

Stories about Bunyan began in Canada—in Quebec or northern Ontario. Scholars say the first stories were based on the exploits of a real, human-size logger who lived in the mid-1800's. These stories spread throughout the logging camps of the American northwest. But when the Paul Bunyan stories were first written down, in the early 1900's, they had changed. The Bunyan of these stories was a giant. And the stories themselves were tall tales, each more outlandish than the last.

One story has it that Bunyan carved the Grand Canyon by accident, by dragging his pick across the ground. Another tells how he built a hotel, with the top seven stories hinged to let the moon pass by. He used a charred pine tree as a pencil. And he invented logging. He transported the logs in bundles that were tied around the neck of his pet—an enormous bright blue ox named Babe. Babe's footprints were so large that when they filled with water, ponds formed. People who fell in could drown. The Mississippi River formed by accident from a leak in Babe's water tank.

Thus—according to legend, at least—the New World, like the old, was shaped by giants.

HIDDEN RIVERS

The Mississippi is one of the most famous rivers in North America. On its banks is an equally famous city—New Orleans. This city was the site of the 1984 World's Fair, whose theme was "The World of Rivers . . . Fresh Water as a Source of Life."

The Mississippi and 24 other well-known rivers of the United States and Canada are listed below (in the left column). Match each to a city that is located on its banks (in the right column). You may wish to use an atlas to help you.

1. Alabama
2. Arkansas
3. Bow
4. Brazos
5. Charles
6. Colorado
7. Connecticut
8. Delaware
9. Fraser
10. Hudson
11. Kansas
12. Mississippi
13. Missouri
14. Ohio
15. Potomac
16. Red
17. Rio Grande
18. Saint Lawrence
19. Snake
20. Susquehanna
21. Tanana
22. Tennessee
23. Wabash
24. Willamette
25. Yellowstone

a. Billings, Montana
b. Boston, Massachusetts
c. Calgary, Alberta
d. Chattanooga, Tennessee
e. El Paso, Texas
f. Fairbanks, Alaska
g. Harrisburg, Pennsylvania
h. Lewiston, Idaho
i. Louisville, Kentucky
j. Montgomery, Alabama
k. New Orleans, Louisiana
l. New York, New York
m. Omaha, Nebraska
n. Portland, Oregon
o. Quebec, Quebec
p. Shreveport, Louisiana
q. Springfield, Massachusetts
r. Terre Haute, Indiana
s. Topeka, Kansas
t. Trenton, New Jersey
u. Tulsa, Oklahoma
v. Vancouver, British Columbia
w. Waco, Texas
x. Washington, D.C.
y. Yuma, Arizona

ANSWERS: 1,j; 2,u; 3,c; 4,w; 5,b; 6,y; 7,q; 8,t; 9,v; 10,l; 11,s; 12,k; 13,m; 14,i; 15,x; 16,p; 17,e; 18,o; 19,h; 20,g; 21,f; 22,d; 23,r; 24,n; 25,a.

Next, go on a hunt. All 25 rivers are hidden in this search-a-word puzzle. Try to find them. Cover the puzzle with a sheet of tracing paper. Read forward, backward, up, down, and diagonally. Then shade in the letters of each river as you find it. One river has been shaded in for you.

Some letters will be left over after you have found all the rivers. Circle all the unused letters. If you read them from left to right, you will find a hidden title for the puzzle.

Y	B	O	W	F	E	E	S	S	E	N	N	E	T
E	O	A	M	A	L	A	B	A	M	A	O	U	S
L	R	I	P	P	I	S	S	I	S	S	I	M	I
L	E	V	H	E	R	A	S	N	O	S	D	U	H
O	D	S	O	O	S	S	S	T	D	U	S	F	E
W	N	N	O	N	O	O	D	L	A	S	A	R	T
S	A	F	A	U	Z	E	S	A	R	Q	S	P	T
T	R	K	R	A	L	E	N	W	O	U	N	D	E
O	G	I	R	A	L	T	A	R	L	E	A	T	M
N	O	B	W	R	S	H	K	E	O	H	K	O	A
E	I	A	A	A	E	E	E	N	C	A	R	M	L
M	R	H	E	R	I	D	R	C	C	N	A	A	L
E	C	T	U	C	I	T	C	E	N	N	O	C	I
T	A	N	A	N	A	A	W	A	B	A	S	H	W

HIDDEN TITLE: Famous Rivers of North America

PARTNERS— PETS AND PEOPLE

You can probably think of lots of ways in which animals help people. There are guide dogs for the blind, companion dogs that help the deaf, and monkeys that help disabled people. Other animals are trained for special jobs, too—horses that pull wagons and dogs that help the police, for example. In Germany, short-legged dachshunds even help the telephone company, by pulling phone cables through narrow spaces.

But did you know that a pet—any pet— can make you a happier, healthier person?

HOW PETS HELP PEOPLE

In recent years, a number of scientists have studied the relationship between pets and people. Here are some of the surprising things they've found:

• Being around a pet can lower your blood pressure. More than 50 years ago, scientists learned that a dog's blood pressure goes down when it's petted. Now they've found

that the same thing happens to the petter. And other studies have shown that blood pressure drops when people simply talk to pet birds or watch tropical fish.

Lower blood pressure can mean a longer, healthier life. One study of heart-attack patients showed that the patients who owned pets lived longer. At first the researchers thought the reason might be that patients who owned dogs were forced to exercise by walking their pets, and exercise is good for the heart. But even when the dog owners were excluded from the study, the results showed that people who owned other kinds of pets—cats, birds, fish, even lizards— lived longer.

• Pets may help sick people recover faster. Researchers haven't yet done detailed studies on this subject. But many doctors have stories of pets who snapped patients out of the blues and helped them get up and around faster. As one researcher described it, "We're beginning to think that it helps many sick people just to have something that is alive. The presence of other life seems to be a stimulus that we need to find out more about."

• Just as animals help people who are physically ill, they also help people who are having emotional problems. One Florida study involved autistic children, who are usually very withdrawn and rarely speak. The researchers took the children several times to play with dolphins at an aquarium. All the children perked up, and several got interested enough to feed or splash water on the dolphins. One boy even began to speak, answering "Yep" when asked if he wanted to visit the dolphins again.

Other researchers have reported similar successes using dogs, horses, cats, fish, and goats. Contact with animals doesn't replace the usual therapy for people with emotional problems. But when people are very withdrawn and don't want to talk about their problems, a pet can help break the ice.

• Pets can help healthy people, too. People who live alone feel less lonely if they have a pet. Pets are companions—especially pets like cats and dogs because they respond to people and are attentive. Studies show that many people treat their pets just as though the pets were other people. They talk to them, and they feel that the pets sense their moods. Some people even confide their deepest thoughts and feelings to their pets.

• Families are often drawn closer together when a pet is in the house. One researcher studied 60 families and found that many of them became closer after they got pets. They argued less, and they spent more time playing together. One woman even cooled family arguments by saying, "Stop fighting, you're upsetting the dog."

Did you know that a pet—any pet—can make you a happier, healthier person? Most people seem to have a need to love and care for something, and to talk to and touch other living things. Children often find that pets can be special friends because they aren't critical and don't make judgments about people.

LOOKING INTO THE RELATIONSHIP

The fact that pets help people seems to be beyond question. But why is it that pets have all these good effects on people? The researchers don't know for sure, but they've thought of many possible reasons.

One is that people seem to have a need to love and care for something. People also need to talk to and touch other living things. When these needs aren't met, people often become depressed. But a pet is always there to fill these needs. A dog or a cat may greet you at the door, and it will always welcome your words or touch.

For young children, a pet can be a bridge between caring for their parents and caring for people outside the family. Pets also provide a sense of stability—when a family moves to a different area or if it breaks up, pets are friends that stay with you. And training a pet can give young people a sense of importance and satisfaction.

Older children often find that pets can be very special friends because they don't make judgments about people. Your dog doesn't care how you dress. A horse won't mind if you failed your math quiz. Your cat will never be bored or critical of your conversation. You can't win—or lose—a game with a gerbil. So people who are under a lot of social pressure find they can relax with animals because the animals accept them just the way they are.

Pets are loving companions for people who live alone. Dogs in particular provide them with a sense of security. And pets can add a great deal to the lives of people who are retired. When people retire, they sometimes have little to do, and they may feel useless. Feeding and caring for a pet helps

such people establish daily routines in their lives. Walking a dog provides exercise. And, perhaps most important, the fact that the pet depends on them helps them feel useful and needed.

Pets are also social ice-breakers. People you'd normally never meet will come up and talk when you're walking a dog. And pet owners always have something to talk about with each other—their pets.

But most of all, pets are fun. We smile when we see brilliant tropical fish darting around a tank. We laugh at the antics of a parakeet or a puppy. And even the most straight-laced person will get down on the floor to play with a kitten. Pets help us relax, and they help us enjoy life.

MATCHING PETS AND PEOPLE

Because of the link between pets and health, many convalescent homes now keep house pets. Others encourage volunteer groups to bring pets to visit their patients. Schools and hospitals that work with emotionally disturbed people also keep pets. Doctors and psychologists often prescribe pets for their patients. There's even a prison in Ohio where hardened criminals are learning to relate to the world by caring for animals—dogs, geese, parrots, ducks, chick·ens, fish, deer, and a goat.

Some animal therapy programs combine physical and emotional benefits. For example, there are horseback riding programs for children who are physically and emotionally disabled. Riding helps the children with physical problems gain co-ordination and overcome their disabilities. And contact with the horses seems to help children with emotional problems open up.

Animals are helping people in many ways, it seems. And more and more people—both families and individuals—are choosing pets. In the United States alone there are about 45,000,000 dogs, 35,000,000 cats, and 8,500,000 horses.

But researchers caution that good things don't happen every time pets and people get together. For good to come out of the relationship, the pet and the person have to be suited to each other. Some situations don't work—a nervous, excitable dog, for example, living with a nervous, excitable person in a small city apartment.

Another important factor is how deeply the person is attached to the pet. When people have to take care of a pet they don't really like, the pet can actually add stress and tension to their lives. Sometimes they end up giving the pet away or abandoning it.

For these reasons, people should choose their pets very carefully. If you're going to get a pet, think about what the animal will need in terms of care, space, and exercise. If you live in a small apartment, choose a small pet. If you're away from home much of the day, consider a bird, a hamster, or fish —none of which will have to be walked several times a day. Remember that any animal can be a helpful partner, if you love and care for it.

Pets are social ice-breakers. People you'd normally never meet will come up and talk when you're walking your dog.

Jon and the Three Wishes

Once upon a time there lived a young man named Jon. Although he worked very hard on his small farm, he was still very poor.

One evening, as he returned from a hard day in the field, he noticed a strange glow on the moor. Tying his plowhorse to a tree and laying down his scythe, he went to investigate the glow.

The glow came from the center of a ring of bushes. Peering over them, Jon beheld a wondrous sight. Many tiny people, richly dressed in velvet green frocks and bright red caps, were dining at tables laden with delicious cakes.

Several of the little people picked up their pipes and fiddles and began to play a tune. Their music was so lively, it set the whole party dancing in the moonlight.

Jon tapped his foot in time to the music, and before he knew it he was clapping his hands. The music played faster and Jon clapped louder until suddenly the whole

party looked up in his direction. Then they vanished—tables, food, dancers, and musicians. The moor was quiet and still.

"It must have been a fairy feast," thought Jon to himself. "They say the fairies feast on these moors."

As Jon turned to go, he caught sight of a glimmer in one of the bushes. When he bent down for a closer look, he found a fairy caught fast in the brambles by her long, golden hair.

The more she pulled and tugged, the more she became entangled.

"Poor thing," thought Jon, and pulling out his knife, he cut her free.

"Oh, thank you," the beautiful fairy said. "If you had not freed me, I would have perished. Fairies can't stand the light of day."

"It was nothing, ma'am," said Jon. "I would have done the same for anyone."

"Nevertheless, you did me a great service," she said. "And as your reward, I will give you three wishes." She then plucked three of her golden hairs and handed them to Jon. "Hold one up at night when the moon is bright and make a wish. I will grant it." Then the fairy vanished.

When Jon reached home, he wrapped the fine golden threads in a piece of paper and hid them under his straw mattress. As it always is when a human meets a fairy, Jon barely remembered his adventure the next day. Soon he forgot it altogether.

By and by, word spread through the land that the king was looking for a suitor for his beautiful daughter, Princess Cassandra.

The king had devised three tests to find the perfect husband for his daughter. The princess' hand and half his kingdom would go to the man who would prove to be the strongest, most courageous, and most truthful man in all the kingdom.

Knights from far and wide rode to the kingdom to try their hand at the test of strength: to chop down a giant beech tree that grew outside the castle wall. Its trunk was as thick as ten men, and its branches spread over an acre of land.

Jon watched as one knight after another failed the test. "If only I could win," he thought. "But I'm only a humble farmer. I don't have the strength of a knight."

A thought tickled his memory. There was a way, if only he could remember.

One day when Jon was working in the field, he saw the lovely princess out for a

walk. It was just as they said. She was very beautiful. Jon stared at her long, golden hair as it gleamed in the sun.

"That's it!" remembered Jon. "The fairy queen's three wishes! They can help me win the hand of the princess."

That night when the moon was out, Jon held up one of the golden strands and said, "Help me fell the giant tree and marry the princess."

There was a flash, and a wondrous axe lay in his hand. It had a blade of the strongest metal and a handle of fine wood.

The next morning Jon stood before the tree. He swung the enchanted axe and brought it down with all his strength. There

was a great crack and groan, followed by a thunderous crash that shook the ground for miles around. The tree had fallen.

Jon was summoned before the king, who praised him highly. But Jon's eyes were on the fair Cassandra, and her eyes returned his gaze. It was plain for all to see that they were falling in love.

"For your next test, the test of courage," announced the king, "you will spend the night in the haunted wood, deep in the forest. If you are still there in the morning when I ride out, you will have proved you are brave."

Upon hearing this, the princess fainted and had to be carried from the room. She knew that no one had ever spent the night in the haunted wood and returned to tell about it.

That evening as the moon rose high, Jon held up the second of the fairy's golden hairs. "Help me spend the night in the haunted wood so I can win the hand of the princess."

Again there was a flash, and he was holding a fairy charm. It was three twigs—from an oak, an ash, and a thorn—bound together

with a red ribbon. Jon tucked the charm in his pocket and started for the haunted wood.

The wood was a dark, foul-smelling place. Weeds grew wild and thick moss hung from the trees, blocking out the moonlight. Strange moans could be heard, and dark wings brushed past Jon's cheek. But he didn't feel frightened. He had the fairy charm, after all. So he curled up under a tree and fell fast asleep.

When Jon awoke the next morning, the weeds and moss were gone. Birds chirped, and sunlight filtered down through the trees. The haunted wood was now a beautiful wood, with flowers growing everywhere.

Jon tied the fairy charm to a tree so the evil would not return, and awaited the arrival of the king.

When the king found Jon standing in the beautiful wood, he could scarcely believe his eyes. First he thought that Jon had come to the wrong part of the forest. But after checking his map, he had to admit that the young man had spent the night in the haunted wood. He had also rid the place of evil spirits.

"You've done a fine job," said the king,

"far better than I had expected. Come to the castle tomorrow for the final test of honesty."

That night Jon held up the last golden hair. "Help me win the test of honesty so I can marry the princess," he said.

This time the fairy queen appeared to Jon and handed him a small cake. "Whoever eats this can only see and say the truth," she said. Then she vanished.

The next morning Jon stood before the king with the small cake in his hand. The princess stood at her father's side, awaiting the outcome of the last test. She had begun to believe Jon would pass it, and they would be wed.

"Now for the test of honesty," said the king. "Answer me this: Did you accomplish the tests of strength and courage all on your own?"

Now, Jon was naturally a truthful person, and he didn't need the help of the fairy cake to tell the king about the fairy, the axe, and the charm.

"You must realize," said the king with a sly smile, "that this disqualifies you."

The princess began to cry softly. But the king looked delighted. Then suddenly, seeing the fairy cake in Jon's hand, he was seized with a great hunger. He grabbed the cake and ate it.

A strange look came over the king's face. Then he, too, began to weep. "I am a lonely and selfish old man," he cried. "I was afraid my daughter would marry and leave me all alone. So I made up a contest with tests so hard that no one could win. But now I see clearly. You are a strong, courageous, and truthful man. Most important of all, my daughter loves you and you love her. I gladly give you her hand."

Not long after that, Jon and Princess Cassandra were married. Since Jon had no kingdom of his own, he stayed on at the castle, and the king was never lonely. In fact, all three of them lived happily ever after.

CHILDREN OF THE OPERA

The curtain is about to go up on another lavish production at the Metropolitan Opera in New York City. The audience has begun to arrive, and the orchestra is warming up. Stagehands rush to put the last props in place. The performers wait anxiously in their dressing rooms, nervously reviewing their parts and making last-minute adjustments to their costumes. But one group of performers doesn't seem worried. They're busy—talking, laughing, watching television, playing games, eating candy bars.

These are the members of the Met Children's Chorus, one of the few groups of its kind in the world. There are about 95 members, aged 7 through 15, all talented singers. And they're some of the coolest professionals to appear on stage. Looking at them, you'd never guess that they're making opera history.

Not long ago, few children were seen in opera productions. There were roles for young people, but these roles were usually sung by adult female sopranos. The children at the Met, however, have changed all that —they've proved that kids can hold their own on stage. Now nearly every Met season includes a solo part for a child, as well as parts for the chorus as a whole. And in the opera *Hansel and Gretel,* children make up most of the cast.

Some of the children joined because their parents are associated with the opera. Others tried out in auditions at public schools in New York. Between 10 and 30 chorus members are used in a typical performance. Each earns about $10. And the Met kids are in demand. They also appear in traveling productions and in operas staged by the City Opera and smaller companies.

On stage, the roles vary. The children may just stand quietly in the background, or they may have more complicated singing parts. Some may be understudies who stand by in case one of the other children can't perform. But it's rare for these professionals to miss a performance. Some are opera fans and hope their careers will continue. Others confess that they'd just as soon listen to rock. But every one of them loves to appear on stage.

These are some of the members of the Metropolitan Opera's Children's Chorus. They are appearing in Puccini's *La Bohème* (above left); Ravel's *L'Enfant et les Sortilèges* (above right); and Strauss' *Der Rosenkavalier* (below left).

THE 1984 OLYMPIC GAMES

The Olympics are the world's most celebrated sporting event. In 1984, however, problems arose. The Winter Games in Sarajevo, Yugoslavia, went off without a hitch. But the Summer Games in Los Angeles, California, suffered from the absence of fourteen nations due to differences between the United States and the Soviet Union.

On May 7, 1984, the Soviet Union announced that it wouldn't send a team to the Summer Olympics. It accused the United States of using the Games for "political aims" and expressed concern about the security of Soviet athletes in Los Angeles. Many people believed, however, that there was another reason for the withdrawal. In 1980, to protest the Soviet invasion of Afghanistan, the United States had led a 54-nation boycott of the Olympic Games in Moscow. Now, it was thought, the Soviets were trying to retaliate by boycotting the Olympic Games in Los Angeles.

All the Warsaw Pact countries except Rumania joined the Soviet boycott. Nevertheless, the 1984 Summer Games opened in Los Angeles as scheduled. And there were more athletes (7,575) from more countries (140) than in any previous Olympics. A special bright spot was the first full-fledged participation by a team from China.

THE WINTER GAMES

The Games of the XIV Winter Olympiad were everything a Winter Olympics should be. Sarajevo, Yugoslavia, located in the scenic Dinaric Alps, hosted the pageant from February 7 to February 19. It was the first time the Winter Games were held in an Eastern European country. There were more athletes (1,510) from more countries (49) than in any other Winter Olympics.

The Soviet Union won the most medals (25), but East Germany took the most golds (9). U.S. athletes earned eight medals overall, four of them gold. Canada won four medals, two of them gold.

Surprises on the Slopes. Five of the eight medals won by U.S. athletes were earned in the Alpine ski races. The first U.S. triumph came in the women's giant slalom. Debbie Armstrong, a 20-year-old newcomer, unexpectedly swept to victory. Teammate Christin Cooper took second place. It was the first time that U.S. skiers had ever won the gold and silver medals in one Olympic skiing event.

The U.S. men were even more surprising. They were shut out in the giant slalom, won by Max Julen of Switzerland, but then they came on strong. Bill Johnson, a brash 23-

Five of the eight medals won by U.S. athletes at the Winter Games were earned in the Alpine ski races. The first gold came in the women's giant slalom, when 20-year-old Debbie Armstrong unexpectedly swept to victory.

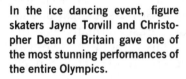
In the ice dancing event, figure skaters Jayne Torvill and Christopher Dean of Britain gave one of the most stunning performances of the entire Olympics.

year-old, charged down Bjelašnica to capture the downhill. It was the first time that an American had won a gold in that event. In fact, Johnson became the first American man ever to win an Olympic gold medal in Alpine skiing.

In the men's slalom, veteran ski twins Phil and Steve Mahre turned in remarkable performances. Phil won the gold medal, and Steve came in second.

Fabulous Figure Skaters. The other three medals won by U.S. athletes at Sarajevo came in figure skating. Scott Hamilton, the reigning world champion, was heavily favored to win the men's singles, and he did. In the women's singles, 19-year-old Rosalynn Sumners finished a close second to the graceful Katarina Witt of East Germany. And in pairs skating, the Soviet duo of Elena Valova and Oleg Vasiliev outpointed the U.S. brother-and-sister team of Kitty and Peter Carruthers.

Perhaps the most memorable performance of the 1984 Winter Games—and certainly the most beautiful—was by Jayne Torvill and Christopher Dean in ice dancing. In their final free-dance program, the British couple performed an imaginative interpretation of Ravel's *Bolero*. The judges gave them twelve perfect scores of 6.

Other Winter Winners. After the grand success of the U.S. Olympic hockey team in 1980, the American squad of 1984 was the focus of much attention and expectation. Although they skated hard, the young U.S. team ended up with a disappointing record of two wins, two losses, and two ties—not good enough to reach the final round. The real power in the tournament was the Soviet Union. The squad from the U.S.S.R. won every game impressively. It defeated a strong team from Czechoslovakia, 2–0, for the gold medal. Sweden defeated Canada, 2–0, for the bronze.

The speed skating competition produced some outstanding individual performances. On the women's side, Karin Enke of East Germany won two gold medals (1,000- and 1,500-meters) and two silvers (500- and 3,000-meters). On the men's side, Canada's Gaétan Boucher won two gold medals (1,000- and 1,500-meters) and one bronze (500-meters). Tomas Gustafson of Sweden won a gold in the 5,000-meter and a silver in the 10,000-meter. Igor Malkov of the Soviet Union won a gold in the 10,000-meter and a silver in the 5,000-meter.

The most individual gold medals by any athlete in Sarajevo went to a 28-year-old woman from Finland named Marja-Liisa

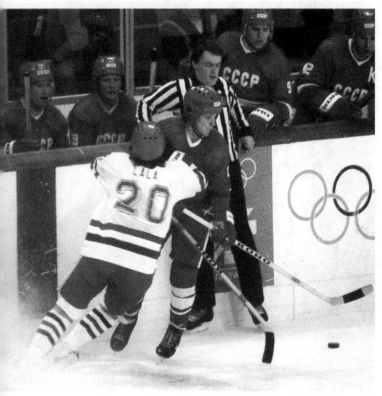

The squad from the Soviet Union (in red) took the gold medal in ice hockey, winning every game impressively.

Canadian speed skater Gaétan Boucher was an outstanding performer, winning two gold medals and one bronze.

Hamalainen. The tall cross-country skier pushed and slid her way to three victories—in the 5-, 10-, and 20-kilometer races. She also earned a bronze in the 20-kilometer relay, won by Norway.

The outstanding performers in ski jumping were Finland's Matti Nykaenen and East Germany's Jens Weissflog. Nykaenen won a gold in the 90-meter jump and a silver in the 70-meter jump. Weissflog, conversely, took the gold in the 70-meter and the silver in the 90-meter.

The bobsled competition featured some exciting runs at Trebević, as well as a controversial new sled introduced by the Soviets. Called the "shark" or "cigar" because of its streamlined shape, the new sled was expected to give the Soviets a slight advantage. It didn't work. East Germany won the gold and silver medals in both the two-man and four-man competitions. The Soviets managed only a bronze in the two-man. East Germany was also strong in the women's luge (small sled) event. Its team took all three medals, with Steffi Martin claiming the gold.

As the Olympic flame was extinguished and the athletes said *dovidjenja* (so long) to Sarajevo, viewers of the 1984 Winter Games could look back on an exciting and colorful two weeks. They could also look ahead to the 1988 Winter Games in Calgary, Canada.

FINAL MEDAL STANDINGS

Winter Games—Sarajevo, Yugoslavia

Country	Gold	Silver	Bronze	Total
Soviet Union	6	10	9	25
East Germany	9	9	6	24
Finland	4	3	6	13
Norway	3	2	4	9
United States	4	4	0	8
Sweden	4	2	2	8
Czechoslovakia	0	2	4	6
Switzerland	2	2	1	5
Canada	2	1	1	4
West Germany	2	1	1	4
France	0	1	2	3
Italy	2	0	0	2
Liechtenstein	0	0	2	2
Britain	1	0	0	1
Japan	0	1	0	1
Yugoslavia	0	1	0	1
Austria	0	0	1	1

THE SUMMER GAMES

The Summer Games of the XXIII Olympiad were held in Los Angeles, California, from July 28 to August 12, 1984. Medals were awarded in 221 events in 24 different sports. New to the Olympic program were synchronized swimming and rhythmic gymnastics, as well as several individual events in established sports. Also on display were two "exhibition" sports—baseball and tennis—in which no medals were awarded.

The various competitions were held at sites throughout southern California. The hub of all the activity was the L.A. Memorial Coliseum. This vast stadium had been built for the 1932 Olympics, also held in Los Angeles. Beautifully renovated, the Coliseum was the site of the lavish opening and closing ceremonies, as well as the track and field competition. For the first time ever, the entire Games were paid for by commercial sponsorships, television revenues, ticket sales, and other nonpublic sources. Los Angeles taxpayers did not have to add a cent.

Partly because of the absence of the Soviet Union, East Germany, and other boycotting countries, the United States won a record 83 gold medals and 174 medals overall. West Germany had a total of 59 medals, including 17 gold. Rumania had 53 medals, 20 of them gold. And Canada took 44 overall, 10 gold.

Track and Field. Track and field competition, the backbone of the Summer Games, featured 41 different events. In front of cheering crowds of nearly 100,000, the host U.S. team took first place in 16 of the events.

Perhaps the most outstanding performer of the entire Summer Games was 23-year-old Carl Lewis of the United States. Lewis equaled the historic feat of Jesse Owens in 1936 by winning gold medals in four events —the 100-meter dash, the 200-meter dash, the long jump, and the 400-meter relay. Another star of the U.S. men's track team was hurdler Edwin Moses. The most difficult Olympic moment for Moses probably came in the Games' opening ceremonies. Taking the official oath on behalf of all the athletes, Moses momentarily forgot the words. When it came to running, however, Moses didn't forget his winning ways. His victory in the 400-meter hurdles was his 105th in a row!

American runner Carl Lewis equaled the historic feat of Jesse Owens in 1936 by winning golds in four events.

Maricica Puica of Rumania won the gold in the 3,000-meter, after the two favorites in the race collided.

Britain had two outstanding performers in men's track and field. Daley Thompson scored 8,797 points in the decathlon—a new Olympic record and one point less than the world record—to take his second consecutive gold medal in that event. Countryman Sebastian Coe also repeated his gold-medal performance of 1980 by winning the 1,500-meter. In addition, Coe took a silver medal in the 800-meter, finishing behind surprise winner Joaquim Cruz of Brazil. Another surprise winner was 37-year-old Carlos Lopes of Portugal, who outlasted the field to win the men's marathon.

In women's track and field, the marathon and the 3,000-meter run were held for the first time in an Olympics. In the marathon, U.S. runner Joan Benoit ran strongly for all 26 miles, 385 yards and won easily. In the 3,000-meter, Maricica Puica of Rumania won the gold. The two favorites in the race, Mary Decker of the United States and Zola Budd of Britain, collided halfway through.

The big medal winner in women's track was American Valerie Brisco-Hooks. She took three golds—in the 200-meter dash, the 400-meter run, and the 1,600-meter relay. Another American, Evelyn Ashford, earned the title "fastest woman in the world" by winning the 100-meter dash. Ashford also earned a gold in the 400-meter relay.

Swimming and Diving. The U.S. team found even more gold in the newly built pool at the University of Southern California. American swimmers touched first in 20 of 29 swim races.

The U.S. women lost only three of fourteen races. Nancy Hogshead won a total of four medals, three of them gold—in the 100-meter freestyle (tied with Carrie Steinseifer), the 400-meter freestyle relay, and the 400-meter medley relay—and one silver, in the 200-meter individual medley. Mary T. Meagher, nicknamed "Madame Butterfly," won golds in the 100- and 200-meter butterflys, as well as the medley relay. And Tracy Caulkins earned golds in the 200- and 400-meter individual medleys, as well as the medley relay.

The American men were also dominant. Outstanding among them were triple gold medalists Rick Carey (100- and 200-meter backstrokes, 400-meter medley relay) and

Alex Baumann of Canada set two world records in winning the men's 200- and 400-meter individual medleys.

American Greg Louganis, winner of the springboard and platform events, was said to be the greatest diver ever.

Rowdy Gaines (100-meter freestyle, 400-meter medley relay, and 400-meter freestyle relay).

Perhaps the top male swimmer of all was 20-year-old Michael Gross of West Germany. Nicknamed "The Albatross" because of his wide armspan, Gross won two gold medals in world-record time (100-meter butterfly and 200-meter freestyle) and two silvers (200-meter butterfly and 800-meter freestyle relay).

The swimming competition was also a rich medal haul for the Canadian team. Canada hadn't won an Olympic gold medal in swimming since 1912. In 1984 it collected four golds, three silvers, and three bronzes. Alex Bauman set two world records in winning the men's 200- and 400-meter individual medleys. Victor Davis took the 200-meter breaststroke. And Anne Ottenbrite won the women's 200-meter breaststroke.

Synchronized swimming, new to the Olympic program, was yet another sport in which U.S. athletes excelled. The team of Candy Costie and Tracie Ruiz won the dual competition. And Ruiz also won the solo event.

Finally, the diving competition highlighted the talents of the 24-year-old American Greg

In the gymnastics competition, high-flying Li Ning of China was a great crowd pleaser. He won a total of five medals (three golds, one silver, and one bronze), including a tie for top honors in the rings.

Louganis. Said to be the greatest diver ever, Louganis far outpointed his nearest rivals in both the men's springboard and platform events. Sylvie Bernier of Canada won the women's springboard. And China's Zhou Ji-hong took the gold in platform. The acrobatic Chinese divers took a total of one gold, one silver, and one bronze medal.

Gymnastics. The gymnastics competition at Pauley Pavilion on the campus of UCLA treated spectators to exciting displays of beauty, grace, strength, balance, and daredevil stunts. And the competition was close.

For the first time in Olympic history, the U.S. men's team surprised everybody by winning the team competition. China won the silver medal, and Japan took the bronze. In the men's all-around competition, veteran Japanese gymnast Koji Gushiken edged out America's Peter Vidmar for the gold. China's Li Ning was third. When it came to individual apparatuses, however, it was the high-flying Li Ning who was most impressive. He won three gold medals and one silver.

In women's gymnastics, the show was stolen by a sprightly 16-year-old American named Mary Lou Retton. In a duel for the all-around gold with Ecaterina Szabo of Rumania, the powerful Retton scored a perfect 10 in the vault and emerged the winner. But Szabo, called the next Nadia Comaneci (the Rumanian star of the 1976 Olympics), led her country to victory in the team competition. Szabo also went on to win three gold medals in individual apparatuses.

In rhythmic gymnastics, a new Olympic event, Lori Fung of Canada came out on top.

Team Sports. The U.S. men's and women's basketball teams were both expected to win gold medals, and they did so in impressive fashion. The men, coached by Bobby

Knight, won their games by an average of 32 points and defeated Spain, 96–65, in the final. The women, coached by Pat Head Summitt, won their games by an average of 33 points and beat South Korea, 85–55, for the gold.

The success of the U.S. volleyball teams was more of a surprise. No American squad had ever won any medal in Olympic volleyball. In 1984, however, the U.S. men took the gold by defeating Brazil in the finals. The women also reached the championship match but were beaten by China for the gold.

The sixteen-team soccer tournament came down to a final matchup between France and Brazil. France won, 2–0, for the gold medal. Yugoslavia took the bronze.

Yugoslavia did even better in other team sports. Its men's squads won gold medals in both water polo (beating out a strong U.S. squad) and team handball. The Yugoslav women also earned the gold in team handball. Finally, in field hockey, the tradition-ally powerful team from Pakistan won the men's tournament, with the Netherlands coming out on top in women's play.

Other Sports. With speed, power, and precise punching, U.S. boxers won a total of nine gold medals in the twelve weight divisions. In freestyle wrestling, Americans won in seven of ten weight classes. Greco-Roman wrestling was more of an international affair, with wrestlers from eight different countries earning golds. China excelled in weight lifting, taking four golds. And in rowing, Rumanian women won five gold medals and one silver in six events; the eight men's races were won by eight different countries.

The 1984 Summer Olympic Games of Los Angeles were a celebration of athletic excellence, friendly competition, and international co-operation. They gave promise for the future of the Olympic movement, and everyone could look forward with confidence to the 1988 Summer Games in Seoul, South Korea.

In women's gymnastics, the show was stolen by 16-year-old Mary Lou Retton of the United States. She became the first American gymnast ever to win the individual all-around gold medal.

FINAL MEDAL STANDINGS

Summer Games—Los Angeles, California

Country	Gold	Silver	Bronze	Total	Country	Gold	Silver	Bronze	Total
United States	83	61	30	174	Portugal	1	0	2	3
West Germany	17	19	23	59	Jamaica	0	1	2	3
Rumania	20	16	17	53	Norway	0	1	2	3
Canada	10	18	16	44	Turkey	0	0	3	3
Britain	5	10	22	37	Venezuela	0	0	3	3
China	15	8	9	32	Morocco	2	0	0	2
Italy	14	6	12	32	Kenya	1	0	1	2
Japan	10	8	14	32	Greece	0	1	1	2
France	5	7	15	27	Nigeria	0	1	1	2
Australia	4	8	12	24	Puerto Rico	0	1	1	2
South Korea	6	6	7	19	Algeria	0	0	2	2
Sweden	2	11	6	19	Pakistan	1	0	0	1
Yugoslavia	7	4	7	18	Colombia	0	1	0	1
Netherlands	5	2	6	13	Egypt	0	1	0	1
Finland	4	3	6	13	Ireland	0	1	0	1
New Zealand	8	1	2	11	Ivory Coast	0	1	0	1
Brazil	1	5	2	8	Peru	0	1	0	1
Switzerland	0	4	4	8	Syria	0	1	0	1
Mexico	2	3	1	6	Thailand	0	1	0	1
Denmark	0	3	3	6	Cameroon	0	0	1	1
Spain	1	2	2	5	Dom. Republic	0	0	1	1
Belgium	1	1	2	4	Iceland	0	0	1	1
Austria	1	1	1	3	Taiwan	0	0	1	1
					Zambia	0	0	1	1

A FIELD OF FELT

It's easy to make a brightly colored felt hanging such as this autumn still life. Felt doesn't ravel or fray, so pieces can be glued rather than sewn. Hangings can be placed anywhere in your home. They can even be used outdoors, as decorations for a party or to announce someone's birthday.

To make this type of hanging you need a large piece of felt for the background and the loops; small pieces of felt in several different colors; two thin dowels; and white fabric glue.

Begin by creating your design. Choose a subject that lends itself to bright colors and that doesn't have lots of fine details. Then "sketch it out," using pieces of construction paper in colors that are similar to those of the felt. Move the pieces around and add or subtract objects until you are satisfied with the design.

Cut the background from the large piece of felt. If you wish, you can glue this onto cardboard cut to the same size.

Use the construction paper pieces as patterns. Pin each piece of paper onto the desired color of felt. Carefully cut out the felt piece.

Arrange the felt pieces on the backing. Then put a little glue around the back edge of each piece of felt, and press the piece firmly in place on the backing.

To make the loops, cut six strips of felt of equal length (eight or more if the hanging is very wide). Fold each strip in half so it forms a loop. Glue the two ends together. Then glue the loops to the back of the hanging.

Sand the ends of the dowels until they are smooth. You might want to paint the dowels, or color them with a felt-tipped marker. When the loops are dry, put the dowels through them. You can then hang the picture by placing the top dowel over two widely spaced nails. Or cut a piece of cord or ribbon twice the length of a dowel. Tie the ends to the ends of the top dowel and place the center of the cord over a nail.

A FROSTED FAIRYLAND

Have you ever woken up on a crisp fall morning to find the world transformed into a glittering fairyland, where diamonds sparkle on every blade of grass? The sparkles aren't diamonds, of course—they're frost, which formed overnight while you slept.

Frost forms in much the same way that dew forms. During the day, sunlight warms everything it touches—grass, leaves, flowers, stones. At night, these objects begin to cool off. When they are cool enough, water vapor in the air condenses on them and forms tiny droplets. This is dew.

If, however, the surfaces of objects cool to freezing or below, the water vapor changes directly to crystals of ice. This is frost, or hoarfrost. There are two basic types of frost crystals. Some are hollow, six-sided columns. Others are flat plates, rather like snowflakes. But unlike snow, frost isn't con-

sidered precipitation. It doesn't fall to earth as precipitation does—it forms there.

After such a night, the first rays of morning sunlight reveal a wonderland. Icy white crystals edge deep green leaves and blades of grass. Bright berries seem to have been dipped in sparkling sugar. Twigs and branches wear armor of ice. And flowers seem to have sprouted extra petals overnight —petals of glittering frost.

If the temperature drops too low, plants can be damaged. But often frost does no harm. This was the case with the damselfly pictured to the right. As the sun warmed the air, the damselfly's diamond-studded coating melted, and it flew away.

Frost is most likely to form on nights that are clear as well as cold. Objects cool off more on such nights because there are no clouds to reflect heat back to the earth's surface. It also helps if there is a lot of moisture in the air that is closest to the surface and if there is very little wind.

ARE YOU SUPERSTITIOUS?

Did you see the new moon over your left shoulder last night? Well, keep your fingers crossed—it looks like you might be in for some good luck. Things don't look so bright, though, if you spilled the salt at dinner or if you broke a mirror recently. Then, some people say, your luck will be bad.

These are superstitions—beliefs based on faith in magic or chance. People who are superstitious believe that certain actions will influence events, even when those actions have no logical connection to the events. Many superstitions date back to ancient times, when people didn't understand why or how things happened. But even though we may know better today, many people are still superstitious.

KNOCK ON WOOD

Touching or knocking on wood is another custom that's thought to help good things happen. This belief has its roots in ancient folklore. In early times, trees were often thought to be the homes of friendly spirits. People touched or knocked on a tree to ask a favor of the spirit that lived there. Some people also thought that knocking loudly on wood would keep evil spirits from hearing them talk about good news—so that the spirits wouldn't step in to spoil things for them.

DON'T BREAK A MIRROR

The belief that mirrors have special magical powers is an ancient one. Early peoples thought that they were seeing their souls when they saw their reflections in lakes and ponds—how else, they wondered, could there be ''other beings'' exactly like themselves? When people began to make mirrors, they thought that the mirror actually held the other self, or soul, of whoever looked into it. If the mirror broke, then, something bad would surely happen to that person.

The ancient Romans added the notion that breaking a mirror would bring seven years of poor health. They believed that life renewed itself every seven years, so after that time a person's health would be renewed. Thus if a person's other self were shattered in a mirror, his or her health would also be ''broken,'' and it would take seven years to get well. Gradually the superstition changed from poor health to poor luck. But superstitions aside, a person in ancient times had good reason not to break mirrors— they were expensive and rare.

KEEP YOUR FINGERS CROSSED

When you hope something good will happen, do you ever cross your fingers? Ancient peoples believed that the cross was a powerful symbol, with the power to prevent evil and bring good. By crossing their fingers when they made a wish, they thought they could trap the wish at the place where the two fingers met, so it couldn't slip away before it came true. At first, two people made the sign—the wisher would hold out one finger, and a friend would place a finger on top to form the cross. Later the custom changed, and people made the sign themselves with their index and middle fingers.

REACHING FOR BREAD AT THE SAME TIME

In early times, bread was considered sacred. It stood for the essentials of life—water and grain (used in making the bread) and the earth and sun (needed to grow the grain). As a result, many superstitious beliefs grew up about bread. One was that it was bad luck to cut a loaf at both ends. Another was that it was good luck to accidentally drop bread—and if you made a wish as you picked it up, your wish would come true. This superstition didn't apply if you dropped your bread butter side down, though—that was bad luck. People also thought that if two people reached for bread at the same time, someone would visit the house soon. And dreaming about bread was considered a sign of a happy event to come.

DON'T SPILL SALT

Salt was hard to get and very expensive in ancient times. If people spilled it, they thought that evil spirits must have been around to cause the unhappy accident. And these evil spirits would surely cause more trouble before they were done. Some people thought that their bad luck would last until they had cried a tear for every grain of salt that had spilled. But there was a way to ward off the bad luck. Evil spirits were thought to always stand behind a person to the left. So if you took a pinch of salt and threw it over your left shoulder, you could bribe the spirits into leaving you alone.

MAKE A WISH . . .

. . . on a star, on the new moon, on the breastbone of a chicken, on the candles of your birthday cake. Each of these superstitions has a long history.

The belief that the stars govern luck goes back to the ancient Middle East, where people thought that each person's destiny was ruled by the stars. If a person was born under an evil star, bad things would happen. But if a good star ruled, it would bring good luck.

The new moon was thought to be a symbol of good luck by people in many places. If you first saw it over your left shoulder, you were sure to be lucky. And any wish made at first sight of the new moon was certain to come true.

The custom of wishing on a chicken's breastbone dates to early Roman times. The Romans sacrificed chickens to their gods and hung the breast-bones up to dry for luck. This grew into another custom—two people would grasp the ends of the bone and snap it as they each made a wish. Whoever got the longer piece would also get his or her wish.

And when you blow out the candles on your birthday cake, you're following still another ancient superstition. Long ago, people lit fires as protection from cold and from wild animals. Gradually any fire—even a candle—came to be a symbol of magical protection. For example, the ancient Greeks and Romans lit candles when they prayed, so that the flames would carry their prayers to the gods. Later, candles were placed on birthday cakes to ward off evil spirits. And today many people try to blow out all their birthday candles with one puff—to make their wishes come true.

Dale Barsamian

THE PIED PIPER OF POP

On a hot summer night in July, 1984, some 45,000 people crammed into Arrowhead Stadium in Kansas City, Missouri. Teenagers, toddlers, grandparents, and people from all walks of life waited excitedly, their eyes on a huge stage that had been erected in the field.

Finally the stadium lights dimmed—and the stage seemed to explode with color, smoke, and light. From the midst of the explosion emerged a group of men, dressed in glittering costumes. But all eyes were on one of them—a slight figure in a silver sequined jacket.

This was 25-year-old Michael Jackson, on the opening night of the four-month Victory Tour he made with his brothers Jermaine, Marlon, Tito, and Randy. (Brother Jackie was kept off stage by a knee operation.) All the Jacksons are talented rock performers. But Michael has become a phenomenon—a pop star who rivals (and perhaps surpasses) Elvis Presley and the Beatles in popularity.

Michael's album *Thriller* has sold more than 35,000,000 copies worldwide—more

than any other album in history. He was nominated for a record twelve Grammy awards in 1984 and walked off with a record eight. Michael Jackson posters, dolls, and biographies are sellouts. And everywhere you look, you see fans adopting his unique style, wearing flashy padded jackets and a single glove.

But what is Michael Jackson really like? On stage, he's all confidence and grace, melting his audiences and keeping them in perfect control. Off stage, he's a mystery. He rarely grants interviews. He's seldom seen in public without a blanket of security guards. At press conferences he hides behind dark glasses and lets others do the talking. When he's not performing, he spends most of his time on the secluded estate near Los Angeles that he shares with his parents and his brothers and sisters. If he ventures out, he's screened by the tinted windows of his Rolls Royce.

Friends say that Michael isn't cold and aloof—he's just painfully shy. Born on August 29, 1958, he grew up in a poor section of Gary, Indiana. Michael was the sixth of nine children in his family. His father, once a guitar player, worked in a steel mill.

It all sounds pretty ordinary—but Michael's life wasn't ordinary for very long. Before he even started school, he was singing with his older brothers—Jackie, Tito, Marlon, and Jermaine. Encouraged by their parents, the boys put together an act and chose a name, the Jackson Five. First they won a local talent contest. Then, when Michael was 5, they began playing in nightclubs. Soon they were on the road, traveling by van from one show to the next. They appeared at the famous Apollo Theater, in New York City. And in 1969, they landed a recording contract with a major studio. Jackson Five hits like "A-B-C," "I Want You Back," and "I'll Be There" started topping the charts.

The Jackson Five continued to record hit after hit, and Michael recorded a few singles, such as "Ben," on his own. Then, in 1975, Jermaine left to pursue a solo career. But younger brother Randy joined the group, and they continued to perform as the Jacksons. They starred in their own television show. And in 1978, Michael made his first solo album, *Off the Wall,* and started skyrocketing to stardom.

What accounts for Michael's enormous popularity? He's a supremely talented singer and dancer, for one thing. But his appeal seems to go beyond his talent. Some people think that his shyness has a lot to do with his popularity. Despite his razzle-dazzle performances, he has a wispy, childlike quality. He comes across as a sensitive person who could be easily hurt. Another factor in his appeal may be his way of life. Unlike many stars, Michael doesn't smoke, drink, or swear. He's a vegetarian. He's deeply religious. And parts of his lifestyle seem to be straight out of a storybook.

Each of his trademark single gloves, for example, is hand embroidered with 1,200 rhinestones. His home looks like a castle. One room is filled with video games. Another room is lined with gold and platinum records. There's a movie theater with 32 red velvet seats. Still another room is a recreation of the Disneyland ride "Pirates of the Caribbean," with mechanical figures.

Michael has his own popcorn cart, his own ice-cream machine, and a "bar" that's actually an old-fashioned soda fountain. He keeps a whole zoo of pets, including a boa constrictor, a llama, exotic birds, and two deer. Sometimes he can be seen riding around the parklike grounds of his estate on a motor scooter or in an electric car.

But the fans who each day keep watch outside the gates of the estate rarely see the star. And the mystery around him has given rise to lots of rumors—that he has had extensive surgery to improve his looks, for example. (Michael's friends and family say that he did have his nose shaped, but that's all.)

Even without gossip, Michael Jackson always seems to be in the news. Early in 1984, when he was burned while filming a television commercial, fans kept a vigil outside the hospital where he was treated. Not long after that, President Ronald Reagan personally handed him an award for helping in a campaign against drinking and driving. Then came summer—and the fabulous thirteen-city Victory Tour. Even at $30 a ticket, it was a sellout everywhere.

The Jacksons say the tour marked the last time that the brothers will appear together. And Michael may branch out in new directions. He's already made top-selling videos of his songs and appeared in the film *The Wiz,* and he says he'd like to star in a movie version of *Peter Pan.* But one thing seems certain—the world will be hearing more from Michael Jackson in the future.

Pop star Michael Jackson (shown here with Quincy Jones) walked off with a record eight Grammy awards in 1984.

LOOSE CABOOSE

The snow started to fall ever so lightly during the final performance of the circus at Corkerville. It was snowing just a bit harder as the roustabouts folded up the big tent and put it aboard Casey Jr., the circus train. And when all the animals and all the circus folk were finally on board the little train, it was still snowing.

Casey huffed and puffed out of the Corkerville station. The next stop on the circus tour was Middletown. "It won't be an easy trip!" Casey thought, as he tooted his whistle and gathered up speed. Casey had made this trip many times before, and he knew that soon the railroad tracks would lead high up into the mountains. It was a tough trip in nice weather. In a snowstorm, it would be difficult indeed!

An hour later, the little circus train started the long climb into the mountains. The snow that had fallen lightly in Corkerville was now a raging blizzard.

Casey strained against the icy wind and swirling snow, his lamp the only spot of light in the midnight storm. Higher and higher he climbed, his wheels slipping and sliding on the frozen rails.

The circus train cars behind Casey were dark. Everybody was asleep, worn out from the performance in Corkerville. In the last car of the train, Timothy and Dumbo were sleeping, too, quite unaware of the storm outside.

Suddenly, as Casey Jr. struggled to reach the top of the tallest mountain, something terrible happened. The coupling that held the caboose snapped. The car that held the sleeping Dumbo and Timothy rolled backward, away from the rest of the train, and down the steep, icy tracks.

The uncoupled caboose rolled faster and faster down the mountain rails, for miles and miles. Then, with a squishy bump, the car halted abruptly.

The bump had bounced Timothy and Dumbo around in the car, waking them up.

"Hey! What's going on?" Timothy sputtered, rubbing his head.

Dumbo blinked.

They both looked out the window, but they couldn't see a thing. Timothy opened the back door of the caboose. Snowflakes and wind blew in.

It didn't take him long to figure out what

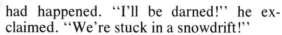

had happened. "I'll be darned!" he exclaimed. "We're stuck in a snowdrift!"

Timothy closed the door to keep the snow out. "The caboose must have come loose," he said. "It looks like we're stranded in a blizzard."

Dumbo didn't look worried. Surely Casey Jr. would come back for them.

Timothy shook his head. "I don't think Casey can come back and get us," he said, contradicting Dumbo's unspoken thought. "Those tracks are covered with snow. He won't be able to back up—his snowplow is just for going forward."

Timothy closed his eyes and thought hard. Then he looked at Dumbo. "I guess you'll just have to fly us out of here, Dumbo," he said.

Dumbo had never flown in a snowstorm before, and Timothy knew that. As Dumbo stared at him in amazement, he joked, "Well, there's a first time for everything!"

Timothy and Dumbo opened the caboose door again and went out on the car platform, in the whistling wind and swirling snow.

Timothy jumped into Dumbo's hat and held on tightly. Dumbo flapped his ears. In a minute, the mouse and the elephant were on their way.

But they had only managed to fly a few feet when Timothy felt Dumbo lurch. "Flap your ears, Dumbo!" he cried.

The little airborne elephant continued to wobble, and they began to drift lower.

Timothy squinted his eyes and tried to see the little elephant's ears through the blinding snow.

"It's *ice,* Dumbo!" he shouted. "Your ears are icing up!"

In a moment, Dumbo and his passenger had fallen out of the sky and plopped down in another snowbank.

Dumbo sat up and shook the snow out of his trunk.

"It's not your fault, Dumbo," Timothy said. "You tried your best. But now I'm afraid that we're *really* stranded!"

"What are you two doing out on a terrible night like this?" said a voice out of the snowstorm.

Dumbo and Timothy looked up.

Standing on top of the snowbank, just above them, was Joe Stork.

Timothy told Joe the whole story—how their car had become uncoupled from the rest of the circus train and how they had rolled down the mountain in the snowstorm.

"Quite a story, boys," Joe said. "But don't worry. I'll get you out of here."

"*You*?" said Timothy in astonishment, looking from the tall, skinny bird to the short, plump pachyderm.

"Well, I know you could carry me," said Timothy, "but Dumbo's not exactly what you would call a lightweight."

"Are you kidding? I just delivered a baby hippo to the zoo! Compared to that, Dumbo's as light as a feather!"

Miles ahead on the tracks, Casey Jr. had stopped. Everybody on the circus train knew what had happened to Dumbo and Timothy.

Mrs. Jumbo was terribly upset. "Can't we go back for my baby?" she pleaded. But the other elephants shook their heads sadly. "All we can do is wait for the snowstorm to stop," they said.

"I'll fly you out," Joe answered, quite matter-of-factly.

"But Dumbo's a pretty good flier, and he couldn't do it," Timothy pointed out. "It's snowing too hard."

Joe thought that was pretty funny. "When you have to deliver babies all over the world," he laughed, "you have to be able to fly in all kinds of weather." And he shook his wings, showing that the snow didn't stick to him.

All of a sudden, the door to the elephant car flew open and in came Joe Stork, carrying Dumbo and Timothy in a baby-bundle. He set them down on the floor.

"Dumbo! Timothy! How glad I am to see you!" Mrs. Jumbo exclaimed.

Timothy told Dumbo's mother how Joe Stork had rescued them.

"Well," said Mrs. Jumbo, "I guess that makes me the first mother in the circus to have the stork deliver the same baby *twice*!"

ANIMAL CHAMPIONS

How far can a kangaroo jump? How fast can a falcon fly? How strong is an elephant?

Experts don't always agree on how far an animal can leap, how fast it can move, how strong or smart it may be. It's difficult to test the performance of animals in the wild. And it's hard to measure qualities like strength and intelligence.

Even so, animal-watchers have come up with plenty of facts and figures about the amazing abilities of animals and how they measure up to humans.

Swimming Champs. In the Olympic Games, a champion swimmer can reach a top speed of about 5 miles an hour. At that rate, the swimming champ would be left far behind by most creatures that live in the sea.

A sea otter can swim twice as fast as an Olympic champion, a walrus three times as fast. Sea turtles paddle along at 22 miles an hour. Dolphins reach 25 miles an hour.

Penguins are the best swimmers among birds. They use their wings as flippers and their feet as rudders as they zip through the water at speeds of up to 30 miles an hour.

Sharks have been timed at 40 miles an hour, marlins at 50, and swordfish at 58. But the fastest swimmer in the sea is the sailfish. A sailfish has been clocked at the record-

breaking speed of 68 miles an hour—about twice the speed of a nuclear submarine.

Running Champs. The top speed ever recorded for an Olympic runner is 27 miles an hour. That's faster than a charging elephant (24 miles an hour), but not quite as fast as a charging rhinoceros (28 miles an hour).

Grizzly bears have been clocked at 30 miles an hour as they galloped on all fours. A house cat chasing a mouse reaches about the same speed as a grizzly. Wolves and coyotes can approach 40 miles an hour.

The fastest member of the dog family is the greyhound, with a record speed of 41.7 miles an hour. The top speed for a racehorse is 43.3 miles an hour. That's fast, but it's not quite as fast as an ostrich can run. In Africa, an ostrich was timed at 43.5 miles an hour. It's the fastest bird on two legs.

Deer and antelope can top 50 miles an hour when they're running for their lives. A pronghorn antelope has been timed at 61 miles an hour. The only animal that can run faster is the swift, sleek cheetah. In one speed test, a cheetah was clocked by a speeding automobile. It covered 700 yards in 20 seconds, averaging just over 71 miles an hour. That makes the cheetah the fastest creature on land.

Flying Champs. Scientists have used many methods to measure the flying speeds of birds. Birds have been timed from the ground by observers armed with binoculars and stopwatches. They've been followed in airplanes, tracked by radar, and tested in special wind tunnels.

The wandering albatross—which has the longest wings of any bird—has been clocked at 77 miles an hour. Golden eagles reach 80 miles an hour. Racing pigeons have been timed at top speeds of 90 miles an hour.

The fastest birds are swifts and falcons. They have swept-back pointed wings like those of a jet plane. Swifts can easily top 100 miles an hour in level flight. In the Soviet Union, a spine-tail swift was clocked at 106 miles an hour.

Falcons can also top 100 miles an hour in level flight. And when these powerful bullet-headed birds swoop down and dive after prey, they may travel at twice that speed or more. To find out how much more, two scientists trained a peregrine falcon to fly in a special wind tunnel. They estimated that the

Swimming champs: Using their wings as flippers and feet as rudders, penguins are the best swimmers among birds.

falcon's top speed during its power dive was 325 feet a second—about 240 miles an hour. That's the fastest speed ever recorded for any animal moving under its own power.

Jumping Champs. An impala can cover a distance of 35 feet in a single leap. A mountain lion can jump as far as 39 feet. But the champion jumper is the kangaroo.

Normally, a kangaroo walks about on all fours. As it speeds up, it starts hopping on its powerful hind legs. A kangaroo in a hurry can hop along at 30 miles an hour. And it can cover 30 feet or more with each hop. The longest jump ever recorded for a kangaroo is 42 feet.

Kangaroos can jump farther than any other animal, but they're not the best jumpers for their size. At most, a kangaroo can jump about 8 times the length of its body. A frightened jack rabbit can jump 11 times the length of its body. And a jumping mouse, less than 4 inches long, can cover 10 to 12 feet at a single bound—more than 30 times the length of its body.

The best jumper for its size is an insect—the common flea. A flea can jump as far as 13 inches. Compared to the mighty 42-foot leap of a kangaroo, a 13-inch jump might not seem like much. And yet that's 200 times the length of a flea's body! If Olympic champions had the jumping power of a flea, they could sail over five city blocks with a single easy leap.

Flying champs: A swift is one of the fastest flying birds. Swifts have swept-back, pointed wings like those of a jet plane, and they can top 100 miles an hour in level flight.

Running champs: The sleek cheetah is the fastest creature on land. In one test, it averaged 71 miles an hour.

Jumping champs: The kangaroo is the champion jumper. It has been known to cover 42 feet in a single leap.

Diving Champs. When a duck dives for its dinner, it may reach a depth of 200 feet below the surface. Another diving bird, the loon, has been known to dive as deep as 240 feet. The best divers among birds are penguins. One penguin, observed through the window of a diving bell, reached a depth of 885 feet. The deepest dive ever recorded for a human scuba diver is 437 feet.

Some seals and whales regularly dive 1,000 feet or more as they hunt for food. They may stay under water for one to two hours before coming up for air. A finback whale has been recorded at a depth of 1,150 feet, and a Weddell seal at a depth of 2,000 feet.

The deepest dive ever recorded for a free-swimming, air-breathing animal was made by a 47-foot sperm whale in the Pacific Ocean off the coast of South America. The whale reached a depth of 3,720 feet below the surface, where it became entangled with a submarine cable on the ocean floor.

Champion Travelers. Few animals, if any, can outwalk the caribou. Caribou spend the winter in the forests of Canada. In spring they head north, traveling in great herds. They walk through melting snows past the timberline and across the tundra to the shores of the Arctic Ocean. They spend the summer grazing in the tundra. Then they turn around and head back to their forests, a round-trip walk of more than 1,000 miles.

Every fall, monarch butterflies migrate from Canada and the northern United States to the Gulf of Mexico and other southern areas. Fluttering along at 10 miles an hour, resting at night on bushes and trees, these frail insects fly 2,000 miles or more to their winter homes. In spring, their descendants make the trip back north.

The longest journeys at sea are made by gray whales. During the winter they live in warm lagoons along the coast of Mexico. As winter ends, they travel north to the Arctic Ocean, a trip that takes three months of steady swimming and covers between 4,000 and 6,000 miles. All summer long the whales gorge themselves on arctic plankton. Then they spend three more months swimming another 4,000 to 6,000 miles on their way back to Mexico.

Some birds cross the equator twice yearly as they migrate between their summer and winter homes. White storks spend the summer in northern Europe and the winter in southern Africa—a one-way trip of 8,000 miles. And golden plovers fly 10,000 miles from their summer nesting grounds in the arctic to their winter quarters in Argentina.

The champion long-distance traveler is the arctic tern, a relative of the sea gull. During the warm summer months, these birds hatch their eggs and raise their young along the ice-free shores of the Arctic Ocean, close to the North Pole. As summer ends, the terns head south. They fly from the Arctic Circle to the seas of Antarctica, a one-way trip of about 12,000 miles and the longest continuous journey made by any living creature.

The Strongest Animals. In official competition, a champion weightlifter can lift about four times his own body weight. A chimpanzee has been known to lift six times its body weight. Chimps are smaller than humans, but they're much stronger.

According to Jane Goodall, an expert on chimpanzees, the average chimp is about three times stronger than the average person. When Goodall studied wild chimpanzees in Africa, she coaxed them into her research camp by leaving bananas out for them. Extra bananas were kept locked away in metal strongboxes, to be used when needed. Two chimps were smart enough to figure out how to get into the strongboxes. And they were strong enough to do it. They broke into the boxes by snapping steel cables with their bare hands.

Gorillas are a lot bigger than chimps. It's hard to tell how much stronger they may be because they don't often display their strength. Scientist George Schaller, who studied wild gorillas, believes that a full-grown male gorilla has "the strength of several men." Schaller has seen gorillas reach into a tree and rip down branches thicker than a muscle-builder's arms.

The American Indians regarded the grizzly bear as the most powerful creature on Earth. When a grizzly searches for insects to eat, it can flip boulders over like cardboard boxes. When it hunts for bigger game, it can break the neck of an elk or moose with a single blow of its paw. It can pick up an elk carcass weighing the better part of a ton and carry it off to a hiding place.

In the teak forests of Southeast Asia, a trained work elephant can lift a ton of logs with its trunk. And it can drag a load of logs weighing 10 tons. As the biggest of all land animals, elephants are also the most powerful. But they're not the strongest animals for their size.

The strongest animals for their size are insects. An ant can pick up a stone more than 50 times its own weight. It can carry that stone up a long underground tunnel and drop it outside its nest. If a big elephant had that much strength, it could lift at least 300 tons of logs with its trunk and carry them hundreds of yards up a steep hill.

Ants aren't as strong as some beetles. Scientists tested beetles for their lifting ability by placing them in little harnesses with weights attached. In these tests, beetles were able to lift 850 times their own weight. A 200-pound man that strong would be able to lift a weight equal to 14 full-grown elephants. And if an elephant were as strong as a beetle, it could lift a Navy destroyer.

The Brainiest Animals. The brainiest creatures on Earth are the great whales. A cap-

Champion travelers: Every fall, the frail monarch butterfly migrates 2,000 miles from Canada to the Gulf of Mexico.

tured blue whale had a brain that weighed in at about 15 pounds. A sperm whale had a brain that weighed just over 20 pounds. That's the biggest brain ever recorded.

Next to the whales, elephants have the biggest brains. An elephant's brain averages about 11 pounds, but the largest elephants have brains that weigh 13 pounds or more.

An average human brain weighs about 3¼ pounds—not much compared to elephants and whales. And yet no one believes that elephants or whales are smarter than humans. A giant brain doesn't always mean a giant I.Q. Brain size is important, but it doesn't tell the whole story about an animal's intelligence. Even more important is the size of an animal's brain compared to the size of its body.

Humans have the biggest brains for their size. An average person has about one pound of brain for each 50 pounds of body weight. An elephant has only one pound of brain for each 1,000 pounds of body weight. A large part of an elephant's brain is devoted to controlling the movement of its big body.

Even so, elephants have plenty of brain power left over for intelligent behavior. The ancient Greeks regarded the elephant as the smartest of all animals. Today, scientists still rank elephants near the top when it comes to measuring animal I.Q.'s. Elephants learn fast, and they have long memories. A trained work elephant can remember the meanings of more than 200 commands. Experienced work elephants will often perform the right act even before they hear a command.

Apes seem to be smarter than elephants. Chimpanzees, gorillas, and orangutans all have big brains for their size. Often, they are able to solve problems that require real understanding.

In one problem-solving experiment, a hungry chimp was placed in a room. A banana was hanging from the ceiling, out of reach. Boxes were scattered across the floor. The chimp looked around, grabbed a box, placed it beneath the banana, and climbed on top. The banana was still out of reach, so the chimp piled a second box on top of the first one. After piling up five boxes, the chimp was able to grab the banana.

In another hanging-banana experiment, a scientist scattered both boxes and sticks across the floor. Would the chimp pile up the boxes to reach the banana? Or would he find the longest stick and knock the banana down? The chimp did neither. Instead, he took the scientist by the hand, pulled him to the center of the room beneath the banana, climbed up on his shoulders, and grabbed the banana. That was one solution the scientist hadn't thought of.

The strongest animals: Insects are the strongest animals for their size. An ant, for example, can lift an object more than 50 times its own weight. Here, an ant is pushing a captured snail.

The brainiest animals: Chimpanzees have big brains for their size and are often able to solve problems that require real understanding. Here, a chimp is being taught sign language.

At one time, chimpanzees were considered the smartest of the apes, followed by gorillas and orangutans. But in recent tests, all these apes achieved similar scores. And in some I.Q. tests, orangutans scored higher than gorillas or chimps. So until further research is done, it's hard to say which ape is the most intelligent.

One animal, the dolphin, may be smarter than any ape. Next to humans, dolphins have the biggest brain for their size—about one pound of brain for each 85 pounds of body weight. A chimpanzee, by comparison, has about one pound of brain for each 150 pounds of body weight.

Bottle-nosed dolphins have become famous as star performers at seaquariums. They seem to enjoy learning, and they can master a wide variety of difficult tricks and stunts. Dolphins catch on quickly. Often they learn a trick simply by watching other dolphins perform. Trainers say that they learn faster and remember longer than any other animal.

Everyone who has studied dolphins or has worked with them agrees that they're very smart animals. But no one knows exactly how smart they really are. It's difficult enough to test the intelligence of our fellow humans. It's even more difficult to understand the minds of creatures such as dolphins. Their lives are so different from our own lives, and their brains work differently too.

Humans live in a world of sight. Our eyes tell us much of what we know about the world. A big part of the human brain is devoted to seeing. Dolphins live in a world of underwater sounds. While it's not possible to see very far under the water, sounds travel clearly through the water. A dolphin gets most of its information through its ears, not its eyes. It has a much larger part of its brain devoted to hearing than a human has. And its brain differs from the human brain in other ways as well.

Since each animal has a different kind of brain and lives in a world of its own, it's very tricky to compare animals by means of intelligence tests. A test that's fair to a dog, for instance, might not be fair to a cat.

Suppose that a dog wanted to test the intelligence of a human. A dog lives in a world of smells. It gets most of its information through its nose. A large part of a dog's brain is in charge of analyzing and identifying odors. So if a dog could set up an I.Q. test for humans, it might ask a person to follow a scent-trail through a forest. The dog in charge of this test would have to conclude that we humans are pretty stupid!

RUSSELL FREEDMAN
Author, *How Animals Learn*

MARK THAT PAGE!

Bookmarks are fun to make, to use, even to give as presents. There are unlimited design possibilities. Here are four types that can be made quickly and easily.

Clownin' Around. The bookmarks shown below are made with posterboard. They are comparatively thick, which makes them particularly useful for marking pages in magazines. To make these bookmarks you need posterboard, white construction paper, crayons or felt-tipped markers, and glue.

1. Cut out a rectangular piece of posterboard. It should be approximately 1½ inches wide by 6 inches long (4 centimeters wide by 15 centimeters long).

2. The design at the top of the bookmark consists of two pieces, a front and a back. First, draw the front design on a piece of construction paper and cut it out.

3. To make the back, place the front design on another piece of construction paper. Trace around it, draw your design on it, and cut it out.

4. Glue the front design onto the top of the posterboard rectangle. Then glue the back design onto the back of the front design.

5. Gift suggestion: If your mother likes to mark recipes in magazines, you can make a series of fruit and vegetable bookmarks for her. If she is more likely to mark articles on interesting travel spots, make a series of bookmarks decorated with cars, ships, and airplanes.

Rainbow Ribbons. The ribbon bookmarks shown above enable a reader to mark several pages at the same time—the ribbons hang free of each other and so can be placed in different parts of the book or magazine. To

2. Give the bookmark a tongue by carefully cutting out a thin sliver of paper in the center. The tongue should be as symmetrical as possible.

3. Using crayons or felt-tipped pens, decorate the bookmark with initials or a design.

Stars & Stripes. To make the colorful bookmarks shown below, you need three ribbons of different widths, stickers or construction paper, and glue.

1. Cut equal lengths of the three ribbons. Glue the pieces together, with the narrowest ribbon on top and the widest ribbon on the bottom.

2. You need two copies of a sticker or of a construction paper design, one for the front and one for the back. Place the designs back to back and glue them onto the top of the ribbons.

3. More ideas: Glue stars or other tiny stickers down the center of the bookmark . . . cut the bottom of the ribbons so they form a point or a slanted line . . . use red and white ribbons topped by a heart for a Valentine's Day gift.

make these bookmarks you need paper, felt, ribbons of equal width, and glue.

1. Begin by drawing an animal or other design on a piece of paper. The design should be at least as wide as the ribbons.

2. Cut out the design. Use it as a pattern to make two felt pieces, front and back. Small details, such as eyes and a mouth, can be drawn on with a felt-tipped pen.

3. Cut three or more lengths of ribbon. They can be of equal length. Or they can be graduated, with the shortest pieces on top.

4. Glue or staple together the tops of the ribbons.

5. Glue one felt design onto the front of the ribbons. Glue the other onto the back.

Paper Clips. The bookmarks shown above are best made from lightweight, flexible paper. Construction paper is ideal. Because these bookmarks are relatively thin, they are excellent for marking pages in paperback books. Use them as you would a paperclip, with the "tongue" on one side of the page and the rest of the bookmark on the other side.

1. Draw the shape of the bookmark on the construction paper, and cut it out.

HAPPY BIRTHDAY

1934   1984

DONALD DUCK

He has starred in more than 150 films, one of which won an Academy Award. His television credits include specials and his own series. His comic strip is carried by 100 foreign and U.S. newspapers, and his comic books are published in 47 lands. All in all, he's one of the most popular and successful entertainers ever. And in 1984, as he celebrated his 50th birthday, everyone agreed that Donald Duck is still a "quack-up."

What makes the dynamic duck so popular? He has certainly got his faults: He's excitable and impatient. He has accidents all the time. He loses his temper, flushes beet-red, and hops up and down with anger. He's a loudmouth (although you can barely understand what he says). And he makes mistakes —big mistakes. In other words, Donald Duck isn't perfect. And this is exactly why people love him so much—he's just like everyone else.

Donald's creator was Walt Disney, who began making animated cartoons in the 1920's. By 1930, Disney had added sound to his cartoons. And sound turned out to be a key factor in Donald Duck's success.

IT STARTED WITH A QUACK

Donald's story begins in the early 1930's, when Disney was auditioning performers to do various animal voices. Among them was a young man named Clarence Nash. He presented a voice described as a cross between a baby goat and a frightened little girl trying to recite "Mary Had a Little Lamb." But to Disney, the voice was pure duck. Nash was hired, and he has provided Donald's voice ever since.

Donald's first cartoon was *The Wise Little Hen,* which was released on June 9, 1934. He played a secondary role: Along with other barnyard animals, he refused to help the hen sow corn—and as a result didn't get to eat any. His second film, a Mickey Mouse cartoon called *Orphan's Benefit,* was released the same year, and in it he was given a much larger speaking (or, more accurately, squawking) role.

From that modest start, it didn't take long for the duck to waddle his way to stardom.

In 1935, he was featured in *Band Concert,* the first color Mickey Mouse cartoon. And by 1936, he was ready to take top billing in a cartoon of his own—*Donald and Pluto.*

As might be expected, the new star soon found romance. In the 1937 cartoon *Don Donald,* he courted a señorita named Donna. She was the model for a new character— Daisy Duck—who was featured in many of Donald's later films. The next year, Donald's three mischievous nephews—Huey, Dewey, and Louie—appeared on the scene. And as the years went by, more fowl characters emerged to round out the Duck family. They included Gyro Gearloose, a wacky inventor, and an uncle, Scrooge McDuck—a jillion-aire who liked to spend his free time relaxing in his vast moneybin.

Cartoon shorts weren't enough for this fast-rising duck, however. Before long he was also appearing in full-length feature films —*The Reluctant Dragon* (1941), *Saludos Amigos* (1943), *Fun and Fancy Free* (1947),

Donald Duck's first cartoon was *The Wise Little Hen,* which was released in 1934.

WRITTEN AND ILLUSTRATED BY THE STAFF OF THE WALT DISNEY STUDIOS

Donald soon found romance—in the form of Daisy Duck, who was featured in many of his later films.

and *Melody Time* (1948). *The Three Caballeros* (1945) combined live-action footage and animation, the first film to do so since some experimental films of the 1920's. The duck also became known for a series of safety and education films.

Donald made important contributions to the Allied effort during World War II. Of course, he was drafted into the Army. His draft notice was dated March 24, 1941, and gave his middle name as Fauntleroy. Donald's wartime experiences were recorded in a number of cartoons—*The Vanishing Private, The Old Army Game,* and others. His most famous wartime cartoon was *Der Fuehrer's Face* (1943), which won an Academy Award as best cartoon short subject. And Donald's own feisty face appeared in more than 400 insignias that the Walt Disney Studio designed for the war effort.

Donald's face appeared on a lot of other

things as well. As the duck's popularity soared in the 1930's and 1940's, shoppers could buy Donald Duck dolls, Donald Duck balls, Donald Duck bread, Donald Duck orange juice, Donald Duck cookie jars, and Donald Duck lamps. There were even cans of Donald Duck succotash. Today the famous duck is still featured on merchandise that ranges from T-shirts to encyclopedias.

And like many famous film stars, Donald tried his hand at other entertainment fields. In 1935, he began to appear in a comic strip, *Silly Symphony,* with other Disney characters. Three years later he had his own daily strip, and by 1940 Donald Duck comic books were on sale. Over the years he was also featured in many books—including a 256-page biography, *Donald Duck,* published in 1979.

When television came on the scene, Donald was ready. He made his debut in 1954, in a segment of the Disneyland series called "The Donald Duck Story." He also appeared daily on "The Mickey Mouse Club." And in 1960, he was honored by a special show, "This Is Your Life, Donald Duck."

A FABULOUS FIFTIETH

At 50, Donald Duck showed no signs of slowing down. He was still active in television, as host of "Donald Duck Presents" on the Disney cable channel. He continued to greet visitors personally at Disneyland in California, at Walt Disney World in Florida, and at Tokyo Disneyland in Japan. In 1983 he had a major role in a short feature, *Mickey's Christmas Carol*. And during 1984 he was hard at work on his latest film, a short feature based on the life of Christopher Columbus. The lead in this film is played by Mickey Mouse; Donald plays a stalwart crew member.

But Donald still had plenty of time to celebrate his birthday. And what a celebration it was!

A special plane, *Duck One,* carried Donald and Daisy on a four-day coast-to-coast tour. They stopped at fifteen cities for airport birthday celebrations. At Disneyland and at Walt Disney World, Donald starred in special musical variety shows and led parades of costumed characters down Main Street through showers of ticker tape. In California, he visited a Marine base and was named an honorary Marine. In Florida, he led a flock of live ducks to a treat—a birthday cake decorated with peas, corn, and carrot candles. There were special celebrations at Tokyo Disneyland, too.

As the world's most famous duck enters his second half-century, he's still in great demand. Fan mail continues to pour in from people around the world. But success hasn't changed Donald. He's still the same plucky duck—bumbling and hot-tempered but full of charm, ready to take on life against all odds. And as long as he doesn't change, chances are that he'll be just as loved 50 years from now as he is today.

Fifty years after his creation, Donald remains the world's most famous duck.

Snout beetle

Diamond beetle

BEETLE-MANIA

A glimpse at the photos on these pages shows that the variety found among beetles is truly extraordinary. And no wonder. There are some 300,000 known species, or kinds, of beetles. In fact, almost one out of every three species of insects is a beetle. They live in nearly every part of the world.

Beetles belong to the scientific order *Coleoptera,* which means "sheath-winged insects." And this term describes perfectly how beetles differ from other insects: They have a pair of thick, leathery front wings that act as sheaths, or shields, and protect the delicate underwings used for flying.

Beetles range in size from the tiny fungus beetle, which is only 0.01 inch (0.25 millimeter) long, to the Hercules beetle, which may be more than 7 inches (18 centimeters) long. They also vary greatly in shape. They may be long and slender or almost circular. Some are sturdily built, while others are delicate. Some are boxlike, and some are flat, almost paper thin. Beetles also have a remarkable range of colors and patterns. Among the best-known beetles are the ladybug, the June bug, and the firefly.

Every species of beetle has its own scientific name. But many are best known by their common names, which are usually based on the insect's appearance, feeding habits, or habitat. Giraffe beetles, for example, look like odd, six-legged giraffes sporting long antennas. And diamond beetles look as if they are studded with glittering jewels.

Snout beetles, as you might guess, have very long snouts, or beaks. The snout is used for making holes in seeds, fruit, or stems. The female snout beetle lays her eggs in these holes.

Tortoise beetles have the kind of broadened shape and distinctive markings that make them resemble box turtles. Another good common name for these insects might be chameleon beetles, for they can quickly change their color to better blend with the environment.

Leaf beetles are often flamboyantly colored, with brilliant, iridescent patterns. But the names of these beetles come from the fact that they dine primarily on leaves. Many are serious agricultural pests. One of the most notorious is the Colorado potato beetle, which has caused severe famines in many parts of the world.

Some of the best-known of all beetles are the scarab beetles, Most famous is the sacred scarab, which the ancient Egyptians considered to be a symbol of eternal life. Images of this beetle are often carved on emeralds and other precious stones and are worn as rings or necklaces. These scarabs are believed to protect the wearer against evil.

Tortoise beetle

Leaf beetle

Giraffe beetles

George and Barbara Bush, and Nancy and Ronald Reagan. President Reagan and Vice-President Bush were re-elected to a second term of office in a landslide victory.

THE U.S. PRESIDENTIAL ELECTION

Ronald Reagan proved himself one of the most popular presidents in United States history in 1984, winning a second four-year term in a vote that was widely termed a landslide. Reagan carried 49 states in the election. The Democratic candidate, former vice-president Walter F. Mondale, won only his home state of Minnesota and the District of Columbia.

The election came at the end of a long and hard campaign that included a historic first: Geraldine Ferraro, a U.S. representative from New York City, was the Democratic vice-presidential candidate. She was the first woman to be nominated for that post by one of the major parties.

The campaign was also highlighted by important differences in philosophy between the two parties. But in the end, most analysts agreed that when Reagan and his running mate, Vice-President George Bush, defeated Mondale and Ferraro, it was the president's personal popularity that carried the day.

CHOOSING THE CANDIDATES

Both parties chose their candidates in the same way. In each state, they held primaries (direct elections) or caucuses (party meetings) to choose delegates to go to a national party convention. The delegates were pledged to support one candidate or another at the convention.

Reagan announced on January 29, 1984, that he and Bush would seek a second term. From that point on, there were no serious challenges to his nomination. The Republican primaries and caucuses were largely formalities. They confirmed support for Reagan, who before his election in 1980 had served as governor of California and had also been a movie star.

But the Democratic nominations were by no means as certain. Early in the year, Mondale was clearly the front-runner. He had served twelve years as a senator from Minnesota and was vice-president under President Jimmy Carter from 1977 through 1980. But seven other Democrats also sought the presidential nomination. They were former governor Reubin Askew of Florida; Senator Alan Cranston of California; Senator John Glenn of Ohio, a former astronaut; Senator Gary Hart of Colorado; Senator Ernest F. Hollings of South Carolina; Jesse Jackson, a minister who was president of People United to Save Humanity (PUSH), a social action group; and former senator George McGovern of South Dakota.

Mondale took an early lead by winning the Iowa caucuses in February. But at the end of the month, Hart scored a stunning upset by winning the New Hampshire primary. Hart went on to sweep the New England primaries, and he also did well in some western states. Mondale was strongest in the Midwest and the South.

Gradually most of the other candidates dropped out, leaving a three-way race between Mondale, Hart, and Jackson. Jackson, the first serious black presidential contender, did best among black voters. He tried to broaden his appeal to all minority groups, calling his supporters the Rainbow Coalition. And he made headlines with two trips abroad—to Syria, where he arranged the release of a captured U.S. Navy pilot, and to Cuba, where he arranged the release of a group of American prisoners. But his efforts weren't enough to catch Mondale and Hart.

The outcome of the race wasn't clear until the last Democratic primaries were held, on June 5—and Mondale won just barely enough delegates to assure him the nomination.

At the party convention, held in San Francisco, California, from July 16 through July 19, attention focused on the party platform and on the choice of a vice-presidential candidate. Since 1892, some 21 women had been vice-presidential candidates, but always for minor parties. Mondale's choice of Geraldine Ferraro, confirmed by the convention, was thus an important first.

The Republican Party's convention was held in Dallas, Texas, from August 20 through August 23. There, too, the party platform was a major concern. Different planks, or statements of policy, were supported by conservative and liberal Republicans. In the end, the conservatives won out, and the platform that was adopted reflected most of their positions.

THE ISSUES

The candidates offered voters two different views of the United States. In his campaign speeches, Reagan stressed recent improvements in the economy. He said that Americans had been better off under his administration than they had been for many years, and that they could once again be proud of their country's status abroad.

Mondale said that Reagan's policies had made life better for the rich, but that the poor were worse off. He said that the United States should be a country where people cared about those less fortunate than themselves. He also said that Reagan's foreign policies were pushing the country toward war.

The Democratic candidates were former vice-president Walter F. Mondale and Geraldine Ferraro, the first woman to be nominated for vice-president by a major party. They won only the state of Minnesota and the District of Columbia.

The candidates and their platforms also differed sharply on some specific issues:

• **Taxes and Budget Deficits.** Mondale proposed a specific plan to reduce the federal government's enormous deficits. It included raising taxes, especially for the wealthy, and reducing government spending. Reagan didn't offer a specific plan. He said that he wouldn't raise taxes, but he supported a tax reform plan that would equalize tax rates. (Under present tax law, wealthy people are taxed at higher rates than people who earn less.)

• **The Military.** The Republican platform called for the United States to be stronger militarily than any potential adversary. Reagan continued to support the military buildup he had begun in his first term. Mondale criticized the buildup, saying it had been done at the expense of needed social programs. His platform called for less emphasis on military strength in foreign relations.

• **Arms Control.** The Democratic platform supported a mutual and verifiable nuclear freeze—an end to the nuclear arms race with the Soviet Union. Mondale criticized Reagan for being the first president not to make progress in arms control. Reagan defended his record, blaming the Soviets for the lack of progress. He said arms control would be a major goal of his second term.

• **Equal Rights.** Both parties said they opposed discrimination against minorities. The Republican platform made no mention of women's rights, and it opposed busing to achieve racial integration in schools. The Democrats criticized Reagan's record on civil rights. They supported affirmative action to end discrimination, and they backed a constitutional amendment assuring equal rights for women.

• **Social Programs.** The Democrats called for more government-supported job training programs and more aid to education. The Republicans said that job opportunities would increase as the economy improved and that education should be under local control.

There were other issues in the campaign, too. The finances of both vice-presidential candidates were criticized. And the Democrats criticized the Republicans for their ties to fundamentalist Christian groups, saying that these groups would influence government decisions such as the appointment of Supreme Court justices. Reagan denied that this would happen. He said that allowing prayer in public schools, which he supported, would promote religious freedom rather than mix politics and religion.

THE CAMPAIGN

From the start of the final campaign, in September, public opinion polls showed Reagan heavily in the lead. Support for Mondale was strongest among minorities and labor groups. The Democrats hoped that having Ferraro on the ticket would increase their support from women, which was already strong. But Reagan had a wide base of popularity in most parts of the country.

The high point of Mondale's campaign came on October 7, in the first of two televised debates between the presidential candidates. He made a strong showing, while to many viewers Reagan seemed less sharp. This raised a new issue—whether Reagan, at 73, was too old for the job of president.

Mondale's supporters began to hope that their candidate might gather enough support to win. But Reagan presented himself better during the second debate, and he seemed to quickly regain the ground he had lost after the first one. (The two vice-presidential can-

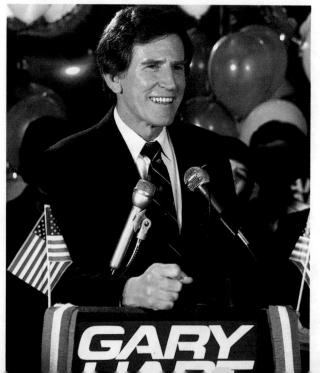

Senator Gary Hart of Colorado proved to be an unexpectedly strong contender for the Democratic presidential nomination. He swept the primaries in the New England states and also did well in some western states.

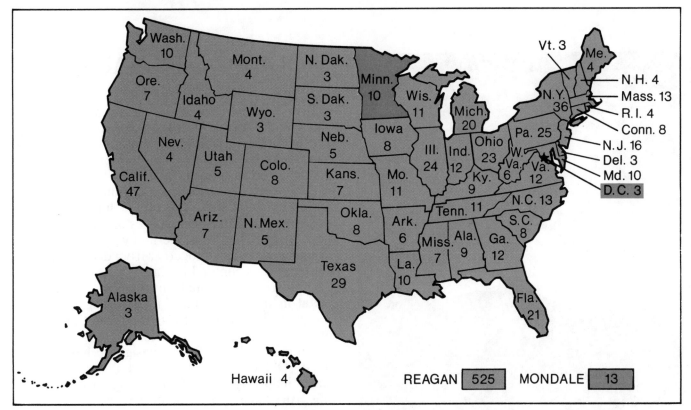

HOW THE COUNTRY VOTED

(The numbers are each state's electoral college votes—270 were needed to win.)

didates also debated on television.) Republicans began to talk of winning all 50 states. They also hoped to gain more than 25 seats in the House of Representatives—enough to be assured of support for their policies. (They already had a majority in the Senate.)

THE ELECTION

In the election on November 6, Reagan won 59 percent of the popular vote. His 49-state sweep gave him 525 electoral votes, compared to 13 for Mondale. Almost 52 percent of eligible voters had cast ballots. This was up slightly from the 1980 election, which had had the lowest turnout since 1948. Reagan drew his strongest support from whites in the middle and upper classes. Mondale got many votes from blacks and low-income groups. More women supported Mondale than did men, but Reagan still took 57 percent of the women's vote.

After the election, Mondale said that he would retire from politics. He laid the failure of his campaign to his lack of appeal on television and the fact that he had bluntly stated that he would raise taxes. The Democrats found some silver linings in the election,

though. Jesse Jackson's primary campaign had succeeded in registering many new black voters. And while Ferraro hadn't drawn enormous support from women, she had broken new ground.

Reagan received more electoral college votes than any candidate in the nation's history. But the Republicans didn't make the gains in Congress that they had hoped for. They lost two seats in the Senate, although they kept their majority. And they picked up just fourteen seats in the House. This meant that rather than getting automatic support for his programs, Reagan would have to work with a divided Congress in his second term. And state and local governments were still dominated by Democrats. In most races, the incumbents—the people who were already in office—won.

For this reason, many analysts felt that the election didn't reflect wide support of the conservative policies outlined in the Republican platform. While the United States had become somewhat more conservative, the vote more accurately seemed to show that the people liked Reagan, and that they were happy with the state of the country in 1984.

MODERN DINOSAURS

Just about everyone has heard of dinosaurs, those mighty reptiles that roamed the Earth's prehistoric swamps millions of years ago. If you've been to a museum of natural history, you may even have seen dinosaur skeletons that were assembled from the fossilized bones of these creatures. But the dinosaurs you see on these pages are a whole new breed. They're modern-day dinosaurs, designed and pieced together from discarded car parts by sculptor Jim Gary.

Gary roams through heaps of twisted metal in the automobile junkyards of New Jersey to find his materials. He doesn't pick up just any car part—he looks for parts with "character" that will fit a design he has in mind. Old oil pans become skulls. Brake shoes help form feet. Leaf springs become ribs. An old car's drive shaft becomes a new dinosaur's neck. The sculptor has even used

the roofs of old Volkswagens to form turtle-like backs for some of his creations.

It can take months or even years to shape the parts and weld them together. Then the new "dinosaur" is painted—often in a startling color, like the hot pink pteranodon shown here.

The dinosaurs have been exhibited in museums from Pittsburgh, Pennsylvania, to Tokyo, Japan. And they always seem to draw a crowd. Many modern sculptors like to use objects they find lying around to create new works of art. But the dinosaurs also make a statement about the importance of recycling: If we continue to waste the Earth's natural resources, they seem to say, we may end up extinct—just like prehistoric dinosaurs.

Perhaps you'd like to try your hand at creating a dinosaur of your own. Look around for interesting objects. Use cans, paperclips, cardboard, paper, fabric, string—your imagination is the only limit.

IT'S A
FABULOUS
FRAME-UP

"Every picture tells a story," says an old proverb. And the frame that surrounds a picture can add to the story. Imagine, for example, a photograph of you and your best friend at camp, rowing a boat across a lake. Wouldn't it look great framed by cattails and a flock of flying geese? And wouldn't a picture of your grandparents on their wedding day be enhanced by a frame decorated with lacy leaves and flowers?

Making unusual picture frames is a popular craft. Decorative wood, ceramic, and fabric frames are sold in many stores as well as at craft shows. Paper sculpture frames such as those shown on these pages are rarer because they are relatively delicate and must be handled carefully—since they are three-dimensional, they cannot be stacked one atop another. Nor can the pictures these frames contain be covered with glass. But the special handling they require is worth it. Once on the wall, framing favorite prints and photographs, they provide a great deal of pleasure.

The main ingredients of paper sculpture frames are imagination and attention to detail. Begin by considering the picture that you wish to frame. What story does it tell? How can a frame add to the story? Suppose, for example, that you want to frame a photo of your favorite rock singer. You could decorate the frame with gold records and black musical notes. The frame for a photograph of your birthday party could be decorated with paper candles and curling streamers.

Begin with a basic frame. You can cut this yourself from a sheet of posterboard or cardboard. Or you can buy a precut mat. Most photo and art supply stores have mats in many colors. Use construction paper for the decorations. Regular all-purpose white glue can be used to attach the decorations to the frame.

You can create the sculptured, or three-dimensional, effects in a number of ways. The most basic way is to curl the paper decorations. This is easy to do. For example, cut a leaflike shape from a sheet of construction paper. Hold the leaf in your hand, grasping one end with your fingertips. In your other hand, hold a pair of dull scissors—the scissors must be wide open, with your hand carefully gripping them in the center of the

two blades. Place the inner edge of one blade against the leaf, and pull the blade over the leaf from bottom to top. If you apply a fair amount of pressure as you pull the blade over the leaf, the leaf will form a tight curl. Less pressure will make it curl only a little. Practice this procedure with various shapes and sizes of paper leaves to appreciate the different effects you can create.

The curling technique works very well when one piece of paper is placed on top of another piece. For example, you can make five broad petals for a flower, curling each petal slightly. Then cut five thin petals from another color paper, curl them tightly, and place them in the middle of the broad petals. The center of the flower can be a star or a circle or a heart cut from yet another color paper.

To give a leaf a frilly look, cut many slits all around its edges. Then remove a tiny sliver, or wedge, of paper along each slit. Next gently curl the leaf around your finger. This technique can be used on other shapes, too.

Another paper-sculpting technique can be used to make cattails. Cut out long rectangles of brown paper, roll them around a pencil, then glue the edges together to form a tube. In the same way, you can make birthday candles or the body of a spaceship.

Try this technique to create a fanlike effect: Using a compass, cut out a semicircle of paper. Form triangles by folding it from corner to corner two or three times. Scallop or fringe the edge. For an even more decorative effect, take a paper punch and make a hole in the center of the folded semicircle. Then when you fan the paper out, you will have a hole in each triangle.

Once you have practiced these techniques, you are ready to begin designing your frame. First arrange your decorations on a "dummy" copy of the frame. (To keep the frame itself clean and undamaged, don't bring it to your working space until you are ready to glue on the decorations.)

This planning stage is the most important step of frame making. As you cut out shapes and sculpt them, you'll find that some things you try just won't look right. But an unusable idea often leads to another, more practical idea. Keep experimenting. If you have difficulty creating complex shapes, such as flying geese or sailboats, trace these from pictures in magazines or newspapers. And keep in mind that it is not necessary or even desirable to sculpt every piece of paper in your design. Some pieces can lie flat on the frame.

Don't glue anything to the frame until all your decorations have been cut, sculpted, and put in place on the dummy frame. Then cover your working area with paper and have a damp cloth handy. Pour a few drops of glue into a dish. Use a small brush or a toothpick to apply the glue to the back of each decoration. Glue only that part of the paper that is to lie flat on the frame. The part

that curves upward should not be glued. For example, if a leaf or flower petal is glued along its center line, it will curve upward on both sides. If a leaf or petal is glued along its bottom edge, the entire structure will curve upward. Both ways are fine—chose the one that looks best on your particular frame.

Neatness is important. Be careful not to put too much glue on the decorations. If excess glue seeps out from under the decorations, wipe it up with the damp cloth. If glue gets on your hands, wipe them clean.

Another type of paper frame is the snowflake frame shown on this page. It's easier to make than the sculptured frames, and it's just as attractive. It is made from paper doilies, which are available in supermarkets and craft stores. Cut out shapes from the doilies and arrange them on the frame so that they form a pleasing pattern. Generally, a symmetrical pattern is best.

Snowflakes can also be combined with paper sculpting. A picture of a snowy landscape could be framed by sculpted evergreen trees and a background sky filled with snowflakes. A photograph of your mother in her wedding dress could be surrounded by snowflakes and pink flowers.

If you want to be especially fanciful, you can make your frame an unusual shape. Nothing requires a frame to be rectangular or oval. Put a graduation picture in a frame that is shaped like an old-fashioned schoolhouse. Put a picture of camp scouts in a tent-shaped frame (complete with sculpted poles). Put a football player's photo in a brown frame shaped like . . . you guessed it . . . a football.

Making these frames takes time. But if you create them with care and thought, they will be a source of great pride and pleasure for many years to come.

PINOCCHIO'S NOSE KNOWS

Pinocchio burst into Geppetto's shop, the door slamming behind him. "Father!" he called out. "I'm home! Where are you?"

"Back here, Pinocchio," answered Geppetto. "In my workshop."

Pinocchio dropped his schoolbooks on the floor and skipped back to his father's workroom. Geppetto was painting something on his workbench. Pinocchio had to stand on his tiptoes to see what it was.

"Oh, what a beautiful little girl!" he exclaimed.

"It's a puppet, Pinocchio," his father said.

Geppetto lifted the marionette off the workbench and danced her across the floor. He had just finished painting her face, and he thought she was one of the prettiest puppets he had ever made.

"What do you call her, Father?" asked Pinocchio.

"Oh, I can't name her," replied Geppetto. "I made her for Mr. Santos, who gives marionette shows in the piazza."

"Oh," said Pinocchio, disappointed. He thought his father had made him a playmate.

Geppetto put on his coat. "I have to go out for an hour, Pinocchio," he said. "Be a good boy while I'm gone, and don't touch the puppet."

"Yes, Father," answered Pinocchio.

"Well, Pinoke," said Jiminy Cricket. "Time to do your homework."

"Okay," said Pinocchio. He sat down to practice his alphabet. But he kept getting his b's and d's mixed up.

"What's the matter, Pinoke?" asked Jiminy Cricket.

"Oh, nothing," Pinocchio answered. "I just feel like walking around a little." He wandered over to Cleo's goldfish bowl and watched her swim around in circles. He sat down by Figaro, who was napping, and watched the kitten's whiskers twitch. He watched a cuckoo pop out from a clock on the wall.

Then Pinocchio wandered into Geppetto's workroom. He ran his fingers along the edge of the workbench. He kicked at some wood shavings under the bench. He picked up one of Geppetto's chisels and put it down.

"Come on back, Pinoke" called Jiminy. "I'll help you finish your homework."

"I'll be right there," said Pinocchio.

Finally he let his eyes rest on the red-headed marionette. She was so pretty.

Pinocchio pulled the puppet off the bench. She crashed to the floor in a tangle of strings.

"What's that?" called Jiminy from the other room.

"Oh, nothing," stammered Pinocchio. "I just . . . er, I just dropped something."

Pinocchio bent down to pick up the new puppet. One of her arms had come off.

Gripping her close to his chest, Pinocchio examined the place where her arm was supposed to attach. The end of a string was sticking out from her body. Pinocchio pulled on it until he had enough to tie the arm back on.

"Well, the other arm kind of sticks straight out," he said to himself, "but I

don't think Father will notice." Then he looked at her face and gasped. The paint hadn't been dry, and her features had become smeared. Pinocchio looked down at his chest. There, on the front of his clothes, was most of the puppet's face.

"Oh, no!" he said, out loud.

"Pinocchio," called Jiminy. "What's wrong?"

"Oh, nothing," answered Pinocchio. "I just . . . um, have to fix something."

Pinocchio climbed up on Geppetto's stool. Carefully, he repainted the puppet's face.

"There," he said to himself. "She's as good as new. He set the red-headed marionette back on the workbench and went to finish his homework.

When Geppetto returned, he found Pinocchio and Jiminy hard at work on capital letters. He took off his coat and went back to his workroom.

Suddenly Geppetto called out. "Pinocchio! What were you doing while I was gone?"

"My homework, Father," answered Pinocchio nervously.

"Is that all you were doing, Pinocchio?" asked Geppetto.

"Of course, Father," Pinocchio replied. He felt a funny sensation on his face, and he heard a little squeak.

Jiminy Cricket looked at his young friend and gasped. "Pinoke!" he whispered, pointing to the puppet's face.

"Sssh!" hissed Pinocchio.

"Are you sure that was all you did while I was away?" Geppetto asked again, coming to the door.

"Oh, yes, Father," said Pinocchio, beginning to write an F. He felt another funny tweak on his face, and heard another squeak.

"Pinocchio, look at me," said Geppetto sternly.

"Pinoke," Jiminy whispered again. "Your nose!"

Pinocchio looked down. Then he clapped his hands over his face.

"I'd say you haven't been telling me the truth," said Geppetto, shaking his head.

"But I have," protested Pinocchio. With a popping sound, his wooden nose peeped through his fingers.

Pinocchio hung his head in shame. "I'm sorry, Father," he said. "I tried to fix her."

"Well, I'm afraid you have caused me a lot of extra work," said Geppetto, "and you'll have to help me fix her."

So after he had finished his homework, Pinocchio worked far into the night, scrubbing and sanding until no trace of his handiwork remained. Yawning, he showed the puppet's blank face to his father.

"Well, Pinocchio," said Geppetto, "I guess you may go to bed. But I don't know what we are going to do about your nose."

Wearily, Pinocchio dragged himself up the stairs. He knew the other children at school would laugh when they saw his nose. He thought about pretending to be sick the next day, so he wouldn't have to go to school. But then he remembered that that would be telling a lie, and lying had already got him in enough trouble. He would just have to face everyone. With a huge sigh, he got into bed and went to sleep.

Later that night, Pinocchio woke up.

Something was strange. There was a light at his window. "Jiminy," he called. "What's going on?"

Jiminy Cricket rubbed the sleep from his eyes. Then he sat up. "I don't believe it!" he said.

"You should believe it," said a very sweet voice.

"Is it you, Blue Fairy?" said Pinocchio. "Gosh, I'm so glad to see . . ." Then Pinocchio remembered his nose. He tried to hide under the covers.

"I see you haven't been telling the truth," said the fairy.

"No, ma'am," said Pinocchio.

"What have you learned from this?" she asked.

Pinocchio thought. Then he looked at her. "It's always better to tell the truth," he said.

"Ma'am," said Jiminy Cricket, "couldn't you do something about his nose? He's suffered enough."

"You're right, Jiminy," the fairy agreed. "He has learned his lesson." And she waved her magic wand.

In a flash, Pinocchio's nose went back to its normal size. "Oh, thank you, Miss Fairy!" he cried.

"You're welcome," she replied. "Now go to sleep, and remember—no more lies."

The next morning, Geppetto noticed his nose right away. "Pinocchio! What has happened?" he said.

"The Blue Fairy came last night," said Pinocchio, "and she waved her wand, and she fixed my nose, and . . ."

"Yes, yes," said Geppetto, impatiently. "And she gave you a pot of gold, too. Pinocchio, why will you not tell the truth?"

"But that is the truth, Father," said the little puppet.

Then Geppetto realized something—Pinocchio's nose wasn't growing. He was telling the truth!

"Well, well," Geppetto said, smiling. "I guess you have learned your lesson."

"Yes, Father," said Pinocchio. "I will never tell another lie."

Jiminy Cricket made a little squeaking noise. Pinocchio gasped and felt for his nose.

"Heh-heh!" chuckled Jiminy. "Just joking, Pinoke!"

CHATTERING TREES

No, this isn't a fairy tale about trees that whisper "Hello!" as you walk by. This is a true story about how trees defend themselves against attacking pests—and how they may even communicate the danger to other trees.

You might think that trees are quite defenseless when caterpillars and other pests are munching on their leaves. But they really aren't. Within hours of an attack by pests, the damaged trees fight back. They change their chemistry by increasing the amount of phenols in their leaves. High levels of this chemical substance make the leaves less tasty and less nutritious, thereby discouraging pests that have come to dine.

In 1983, scientists studying Sitka willows made an exciting observation. They found that when some willows were attacked by pests, other nearby willows also started to increase the amount of phenols in their leaves—as if in preparation for an attack. By the time insects reached these trees, the leaves were filled with phenols. Many scientists now think that trees under attack can somehow communicate the danger to their neighbors.

How do trees communicate? No evidence was found that the roots had carried the message—the root systems of the willows weren't touching one another. It may be that trees give off a chemical substance that travels through the air to other trees. If so, the chemical may be a gas called ethylene. Damaged trees give off more ethylene than undamaged trees.

Another group of scientists tried to find out more about how trees communicate. They worked with seedlings (very young plants) of poplar and sugar maple trees. They grew the seedlings in sealed containers. Each container held several seedlings. But the seedlings were in separate pots, so there was no direct contact between the plants. They shared only the same air.

The scientists played the role of "pest." They tore the leaves of some seedlings. Within 52 hours, the level of phenols had doubled in those seedlings' leaves. This wasn't surprising. The undamaged seedlings, however, had increased their phenols by 58 percent!

The air in the containers was tested, but the scientists weren't able to find ethylene or any other chemical messenger. This didn't mean that such a messenger wasn't there—better equipment may be needed to detect it.

Even if the chemical that acts as the messenger is found, many questions will remain. How do trees produce the chemical messenger? How do neighboring trees detect it? Do all trees give off chemical messengers? As you see, there is still much to learn about the trees that share this planet with us.

THE GREENHOUSE EFFECT

You probably know the story of Chicken Little, who warned everyone: "The sky is falling! The sky is falling!" That alarming warning wasn't true. Today, some people are warning: "The ice caps will melt! The ice caps will melt!" *This* prediction, however, just might come true.

The polar ice caps may melt because the Earth is going to get warmer. Many scientists have predicted this warming trend for a long time. In late 1983, two major reports confirmed the trend—but implied that the warm-up may happen more quickly than expected. One report, in fact, predicted major changes in climate by the end of the century.

This warming trend is known as the "greenhouse effect." It is caused by rising levels of carbon dioxide in the Earth's atmosphere. A greenhouse lets in sunlight and then traps the heat. It's warm inside a greenhouse even on a cold day. Carbon dioxide in the atmosphere acts much like the glass in a greenhouse. It allows sunlight to pass through the air, but it doesn't let the heat escape back into space.

Carbon dioxide makes up only a tiny percentage of the atmosphere. But there's enough of it to keep our planet at an average temperature of about 60°F (15°C). The amount of carbon dioxide in the Earth's atmosphere has been increasing, however. The gas is released into the air by the burning of fossil fuels (oil, gas, and coal), primarily by industries and automobiles. Each year, more than five billion tons of carbon dioxide enter the atmosphere. The gas accumulates, forming a kind of "thermal blanket" around the Earth—and trapping more and more heat. This causes the temperature to rise.

So far, the effects of the thermal blanket have been difficult to measure. But scientists feel that an increase of even a few degrees could have major effects on Earth. Weather patterns could change. Some areas might receive more rain, making the land more fertile. Areas that are now farmlands might turn into deserts. Temperature increases in the polar regions would cause the polar ice caps to melt rapidly. The level of the sea would then rise, resulting in severe flooding of coastal areas.

No one is sure if anything truly catastrophic will actually happen. Most scientists believe that if we can't prevent the greenhouse effect, we can prepare for it— and find ways to deal with the effects.

The "greenhouse effect" is caused by high levels of carbon dioxide in the atmosphere. This accumulation stops the sun's heat from escaping back into space, thus causing the temperature to rise.

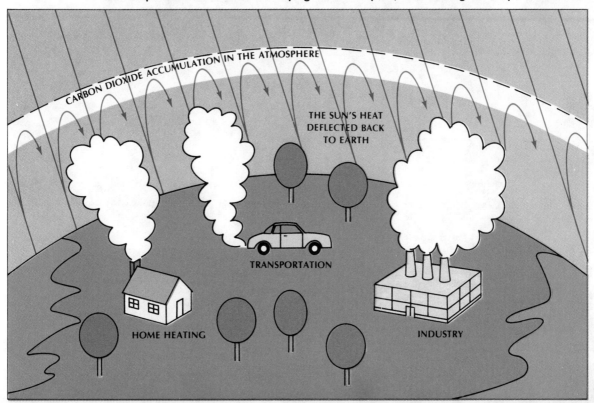

CAPITAL CHILDREN'S MUSEUM

"I hear and forget, I see and remember, I do and understand," goes an old Chinese proverb. This proverb is the fitting motto of the Capital Children's Museum, in Washington, D.C.—a museum where almost everything is designed to be touched, used, and played with.

In the museum's various exhibits, you can "talk" with a computer, pretend to drive a car or a bus, telephone your friends in another part of the museum, weigh yourself on a metric scale, and grind corn to make your own tamales and tortillas. Everything in the museum is scaled to children's size—all the exhibits are easy to reach and see. As the museum's director explains it, "We've taken the concept of learning through doing, of having kids play with things, handle them, test them, as far as we possibly can."

When the museum began in the mid-1970's, it was housed in four rooms of a Washington elementary school. It grew so quickly that by 1978 it had to look for a larger home. A year later the museum opened its doors at a former convent on Capitol Hill.

Since then it has continued to grow, and today there are three main exhibit areas: Communication, Changing Environments, and International Hall. There is also a fourth area, the Future Center. This is a classroom equipped with 20 microcomputers, where the museum teaches computer programming.

MESSAGES PAST AND PRESENT

The Communication area is the newest and one of the most exciting areas in the museum. The basic idea of this area is to show how people have communicated with each other from ancient times to the present —and also to take a look at some of the communications technology of the future.

You start by walking past a colorful mural —drawn by a computer—to a replica of an ice-age cave. Water drips down the walls of the cave, and you can hear the sound of wolves howling. A sound-and-light show begins, and you see that the cave walls are covered with paintings like those made by Stone Age people. Long before writing was invented, people used drawings like these to record information about hunting, tools, and perhaps even their religion.

The Communication area at the Capital Children's Museum shows how people have communicated with each other through the ages. First you will come upon ice-age cave paintings—possibly the first form of communication.

Beyond the cave is a section called "How We Communicate," which shows how to use codes to send messages. Typewriters, telephones, television screens, and computers explain codes that range from pig Latin to sign language. You can learn how ships communicate at sea by using naval signal lamps to flash Morse code. You can also find out how people used codes in ancient times—by signaling with torches, as the ancient Greeks did, or with African drums.

In the Scriptorium next door, you can write with a quill pen. Then you can contrast this method of communication with printing. There is a working model of an 18th-century printing press, and the museum holds workshops on printing and papermaking.

The photography section of the Communication area gives you a chance to make your own slides and filmstrips. You can also see a hologram, a three-dimensional picture made by laser beams. And if you've ever wondered what the inside of a camera looks like, you can find out—by walking right through a giant replica of one. This section of the museum also contains the facade, or front, of an old-time nickelodeon—an early movie theater. If you walk inside, you can see your silhouette projected and captured for a few seconds on a chemically treated wall.

Then climb upstairs through the Tower of Babel—a staircase with speakers that let you hear languages from all over the world. A working model of a communications satellite hangs from the ceiling at the top of the stairs. You can operate a miniature Earth station to bounce messages off the satellite to the other side of the room. The museum also has a real satellite dish outside. It picks up television signals from more than 40 cable stations that you can tune in on TV sets inside.

All the exhibits on this upper floor deal with telecommunications. In one section, you can learn all about telephones. All the telephones on display work—some play recorded messages on the history of telephones, and others are connected to each other by space-age fiberoptic cables. You can use these phones to talk to your friends in the museum. You can also hook up calls on a working model of a 1910 switchboard.

There is also a working radio station, where the museum holds workshops. But the most popular part of the Communication section is the computer exhibit.

You enter this exhibit by walking past a replica of a giant 1950's computer. A videotape shows a scientist of that time performing a calculation with the computer. Then you see a tiny microcomputer of today—the kind many people have at home—do the same problem in a fraction of the time.

Inside the exhibit room, microcomputers are set up for you to use. One computer is called Wisecracker. It calls out to you with a voice synthesizer, inviting you to come over and "talk." This computer will "speak" words typed into it, but only if you type the words phonetically.

Other computers let you draw pictures, tap into a database, compose music, and play games. One takes you through the steps in launching a communications satellite. You can also find out something about the inner workings of these marvelous machines, through an exhibit that gives you a close-up look at a computer's tiny memory chip.

The computers are the final exhibit in the Communication area. They're the modern version of the cave paintings that began your tour—the newest of the many ways that people through the ages have found to record information.

The Simple Machines room is filled with working models of basic machines that you can operate yourself—such as these pulleys.

THE OTHER EXHIBIT AREAS

Changing Environments is especially popular with younger children. This section of the museum explains many things that people meet in everyday life. In the City Room, for example, you can pop through a manhole in a city street to see the pipes and cables that supply buildings with water, gas, and electricity. On the street itself are a bus and a car that you can pretend to drive and life-size phone booths with working phones. You can work in a real kitchen, visit an eye doctor's office, and dress up as a fireman, a postal carrier, or a traffic cop.

In Metricville, you can measure and weigh yourself and other objects in meters and kilograms instead of feet and pounds. The exhibit includes a metric store where vegetables can be bought—by the kilogram, of course. There is also a computer game called Centimeter Eater, in which you try to guess the length of a line in centimeters before an inch worm munches it up.

In the Simple Machines room, you will see how basic machines work and how they can be combined to make more complicated machines. It's filled with working models that you can operate yourself. There are hoists and pulleys that lift concrete blocks, and a model Archimedian screw that bails water from a tank. You can tinker with a typewriter or play on a set of swings that balance like scales.

There are other exhibits in Changing Environments, too. Pattern and Shape uses puzzles, building blocks, and geometric objects to explain math concepts. The Living Room is an exhibit you make yourself. It's filled with objects—foam rubber, fishnets, plastic pipes, and more—that you can rearrange to suit your own ideas. The Factory is an automated garment factory, where you can see how clothes are made.

International Hall focuses on Mexico, and visiting this exhibit is like taking a trip to a Mexican village. There is a chapel with tall arches and columns, a public square with trees and a tile fountain, and a straw market where you can dress up in Mexican clothes. Mexican music fills the air. You can visit a Mexican post office and a turquoise-colored grocery store that sells Mexican food. You can feed a goat or draw water from a well.

A visit to International Hall is like strolling through a Mexican village. You can do such things as grind chocolate with a mortar and pestle and play with Rosie the goat.

There is also a replica of a log house with a sod floor, where you can grind corn into meal and cook it on a little stove.

In a city filled with museums, the Capital Children's Museum is unique. You don't just see and hear the exhibits—you touch them, taste them, try them on, and use them. Visitors to this museum truly learn by doing—and by having fun.

99

The cars of the future will be sleek, smooth, comfortable, and computerized.

CARS OF THE FUTURE

A pod-like city car with rear wheels that can be steered, to slip into tight parking spots . . . a three-wheeler that seats two people . . . a car with computerized sensors that detect objects in its path . . . an "outrigger" car with wheels that extend from its body at slow speeds and are drawn in close to the body at high speeds.

These are just a few of the cars that you may see driving down the highway in the not too distant future. They're on designers' drawing boards right now. They're smooth and sleek and shiny, and some of them almost look as though they could take off from the highway and head for outer space.

The designs are based on some trends that can be seen now. There are more and more people in the world, but families are getting smaller. This means that in the future there may be more cars, each carrying fewer people. People are also more concerned with safety and comfort in their cars. And our supplies of fuel are running low.

With these trends in mind, some designers think that the cars of the future will fall into several distinct types. There will be little three-wheeled, one- or two-passenger commuter cars, designed to go as far as 75 miles (120 kilometers) on each gallon of gasoline. There will be slightly larger versions that seat three people abreast. And there will be low-slung, sleek vans to replace the station wagons and boxy vans of today. Some designers envision a basic three-seater that can be attached to various rear ends, to become a truck, a van, or a larger passenger car.

All the cars will be rounder and smoother in shape. The sleek shapes will have a purpose: They'll cut wind resistance at high speeds and therefore save fuel. The cars will save fuel in other ways, too. They'll be lighter, with more parts made of tough, space-age plastics and ceramics. Some cars of the future may even burn alcohol or natural gas instead of gasoline.

Lots of comfort and convenience features are already built into cars. But tomorrow's cars will have even more. For example, your car might have a replaceable engine that pops out for easy servicing. You could drop the engine off at the service station and plug in a spare engine while it's being tuned up.

But the greatest advances in convenience and safety will come from computers that will be built right into cars. Some computers will constantly monitor the car's engine, brakes, and electrical systems. If your oil is low or your turn signals aren't working, the computer will tell you—often in a human voice! It will also tell you your speed, how much fuel you have, and how far you have to go to your destination. Other computers will adjust your seat and tune your radio automatically. You may even be able to tell them what to do just by speaking to them. Door and ignition locks may be keyless and respond to computer passwords.

Cars may be equipped with radar that can sense objects in their paths or with special sensors that follow guiding marks built into roadways. The sensors would be connected to the car's steering and brakes, so the car would stay safely on course.

The dashboard of the future car may be equipped with a video screen. The screen

could take the place of a rear-view mirror and show what's behind the car. It might also display the owner's manual. Or the car's computer could communicate with a satellite that would radio back your position. The position would be shown on a video map, so you'd know exactly where you were. The satellite could also radio for help if you had trouble on the road.

What will the cars of the future really be like? No one knows for sure. But if the designers' visions come true, they're certain to be exciting.

TOMORROW'S DESIGNERS

The cars of the future are getting ready to roll— in the studios of a school in Pasadena, California. The school is the Art Center College of Design. It has trained more professional automobile designers than any other school in the world.

The college was founded in 1930 in Los Angeles. Today it's housed in modern buildings set in parklike surroundings. There, students who are majoring in transportation design complete a four-year program that includes academic studies as well as studio courses.

The students design more than cars—in some courses, they put their felt-tipped pens to work on vehicles that range from space capsules to motorcycles. But cars are the focus of the program. At the end of the line is a bachelor's degree and, in all likelihood, a job on the design staff of a major car maker. The chances are strong that at least some of the cars of the future will have their start on drawing boards in Pasadena.

This 3-wheeled commuter will get 75 miles to the gallon.

YOUNG PHOTOGRAPHERS

Is photography a form of magic? So it would seem from the pictures shown here. In some, the magic is obvious—double exposures have put a human being in a tiny jar and brought a computer to life. In other pictures, the magic is more subtle. The photographers—all young people—have found new beauty and texture in simple objects and everyday scenes.

These pictures were among the winners in the 1984 Scholastic/Kodak Photo Awards Program. The contest is open to junior and senior high school students in the United States and Canada, and it offers scholarships and other awards. Even without the contest, though, photography provides young people with something special—the chance to practice a bit of magic.

Jarred Up, by Lance Moritz, 17, Havelock, North Carolina

Togetherness, by Jeff Kozlowski, 17, Wausau, Wisconsin

Untitled, by Kerry Green, 17, Lakewood, Colorado

Untitled,
by Andrew Ward, 16,
Oakland, California

Self Programming Computer,
by William Evans, 18,
Anaheim, California

Blinded,
by Tyler Smith, 17,
Naples, Florida

Untitled,
by Sean Oertle, 17,
Provo, Utah

Sea otter

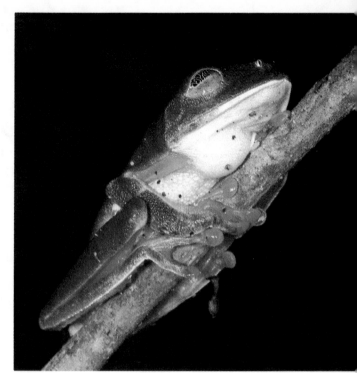

Tree frog

DO NOT DISTURB

If you're like most people, you spend at least a third of every day sleeping. During sleep, muscles relax, heartbeat and breathing slow down, and you gradually lose awareness of your surroundings. Sleep lets your body rebuild energy after a busy day.

Just like you, most animals need periods of sleep each day. But you might find some of their sleeping habits—and their bedrooms—surprising. A tree frog, for example, will fall asleep in the middle of the day, right in the branches of a tree. Like most amphibians, the tree frog sleeps very lightly and doesn't dream. The slightest noise will awaken it. Birds and mammals sleep more deeply. Mammals dream, and scientists think that birds may have very short dreams, too.

Some animals can sleep almost anywhere. Sea lions stretch out and doze off on a bed of hard rocks. Another ocean-loving animal, the sea otter, likes to float lazily on its back and be rocked to sleep by the waves. Before it goes to sleep, a sea otter will wrap strands of seaweed called kelp around its body. The kelp looks like it's being used as a blanket, but it's not. It acts as an anchor that keeps the sea otter from drifting away with the ocean currents.

Koala

Many birds fall asleep while firmly grasping a tree branch, often with one leg. Most birds are active during the day and doze in the trees at night. But some birds, such as owls, are nocturnal—they sleep during the day and hunt for food at night.

The koala also sleeps during the day, cradled in the branches of a eucalyptus tree. This tree provides the koala not only with a bed but also with dinner—its leaves are the Australian animal's only food.

Some animals are super sleepers—they hibernate during the cold winter months. Hibernation is different from true sleep. The animal's heartbeat and breathing slow down much more than they do in sleep, and its body temperature drops. This means that the animal uses much less energy, and it can live for months on fat stored in its body.

The dormouse is a famous hibernator—in fact, its name is thought to come from the French word *dormir,* which means "to sleep." The dormouse prepares for winter by eating as much as it can and getting fat. Then it curls up in a snug den and snoozes the winter away. When it wakes up in the spring, it may weigh only half what it weighed in the fall.

A famous literary dormouse was a guest at the Mad Hatter's tea party in *Alice's Adventures in Wonderland.* And, as you may have guessed, it spent most of the time dozing over its teacup!

Sea lions

Saw-whet owl

Dormouse

FUN & GAMES

The year is 1984—B.C. The sun is setting slowly in the western desert, and a cool breeze has sprung up. The waters of the Nile lap gently against the riverbank. Inside their house, the members of an Egyptian family light their oil lamps and talk quietly among themselves. How will they spend this cool and peaceful evening?

They'll play a board game, just as you might on a similar night at home. People were playing board games as long ago as 3000 B.C., and some of their games remained popular for thousands of years. In fact, some games that *you* play may be thousands of years old.

At different times and in different places, different games became something of a passion with people. They spent hours playing them—and sometimes small fortunes on elaborate pieces and boards. The games they made were not just ways to spend free time. They were works of art. And even when an ancient game is no longer played, the boards and pieces may still exist.

GAMES OF THE ANCIENT MIDEAST

The most popular game of ancient Egypt seems to have been senet, which means "passing." Archeologists have found stone boards that were used to play this game about 4,000 years ago. And they've found evidence that the game was popular for more than 2,000 years, not just in Egypt but throughout the Middle East.

What the archeologists haven't found is how to play the game. Senet boards can be bought today. But the rules of the modern game were thought up by people who studied the ancient Egyptians and guessed about how they might have played it.

Senet was played on a board with three rows of ten spaces each. Some people think the game may have had some religious or philosophical meaning. One theory has it that as players moved their pieces from space to space, they duplicated the journey of a soul through the underworld.

Senet seems to have found favor with people in all walks of life. Some senet boards have been found scratched onto tombs and temples, showing that workers in these buildings probably played it. Peasants probably drew senet boards in the sand and used pebbles for pieces. But royalty played on boards of rare woods and ivory. The tomb of the pharoah Tutankhamen contained four such boards, each perfectly preserved.

GAMES OF STRATEGY

The Asian game Go, or Wei-Chi, may hold the title as the world's longest-lived game. Go originated in China about 2300 B.C., and it is still played by millions of people in China, Japan, and elsewhere in Asia.

Go can be described as a game of warfare. It is played on a grid, which is empty at the start of the game. The two players place small black or white pieces on the grid, each trying to encircle and capture the other's pieces. The game sounds simple—but Go is actually one of the most complicated games ever invented. Masters of the game were honored as wise men in ancient China. And until 1600, students at Japan's military academy were taught the game as a way of learning military strategy.

Go is also played in Western countries. But a game of strategy that you may be more familiar with is chess. Chess originated in India in the 500's and then spread to Persia.

Senet was the most popular game of ancient Egypt, and it was played by people from all walks of life. Royalty played on boards of rare woods and ivory. The senet games above were found in the tomb of the pharoah Tutankhamen. Below, Japanese men play Go, which may hold the title as the world's longest-lived game. It originated in China about 2300 B.C. and is still played by millions of people.

Pachisi, India's national game, has been played there for centuries. It became popular in Europe in the 1800's, and several versions were developed. One version popular in Germany was called *chinesenspiel* (left)—a game for children in which small Chinese figures were used as the playing pieces.

It was brought to Europe by the Arabs, and there the game won lasting popularity. One story recounts that when King John of England was besieged in the city of Rouen in 1204, he refused to see to the city's defense until he had finished a long-running game of chess.

As the game developed in Europe, chess mirrored not only battle but society. The playing pieces—kings, queens, knights, castles, bishops, and pawns—were often carved and painted in great detail to show people from society's different levels. And the boards themselves were often inlaid with ivory and other precious materials.

Checkers, a much simpler game, was played with pieces that were no less beautiful. The checkers themselves were often carved with various designs, and Queen Elizabeth I of England played on an emerald-studded board. The origins of checkers are unclear. But one school of thought believes that it was developed in medieval Europe, using the board of chess and the pieces from another game, backgammon.

GAMES OF SKILL—AND LUCK

In backgammon, players need luck as well as skill—they move their pieces around the board according to the roll of dice. Back-gammon is one of the world's most ancient games. It was probably brought to Europe from the Middle East by the Crusaders in the early 1100's. And it has been played in many countries under many names—*tric-trac* in France, *puff* in Germany, *tarola reale* in Italy. The English name is said to come either from the Welsh words *back* and *gammon* ("little battle") or the Saxon words *bac* and *gamen* ("back game").

Backgammon has been popular for centuries in India, and it is thought to have been the forerunner of India's national game—pachisi. In this game, the pieces move around a cross-shaped board as dictated by throws of cowrie-shells. The pachisi board built by the Moghul emperor Akbar in the 1500's may have been the most elaborate game board ever made. It was built to human scale and inlaid with marble—and the playing pieces were slaves from Akbar's harem.

Pachisi became popular in Europe in the 1800's, and several versions were developed. One version popular in Germany was *chinesenspiel*—a simplified game for children in which small Chinese figures were the playing pieces. A popular version today played in Western countries is Parcheesi, which uses a somewhat different board and regular dice.

110

Another game that requires a bit of luck is dominoes, which is played with flat, oblong blocks. Players try to match the number of dots on the blocks they hold with the dots on blocks that have already been played. This game was known in the 1700's in Italy, but its actual origins have never been definitely established.

Mah-jongg is a very old Chinese game that may have developed from dominoes. It is played with ivory tiles that bear colorful pictures and symbols. This game was all the rage in the United States in the 1920's, and even today it has a number of enthusiasts. The game is very popular in Japan, where many towns have mah-jongg parlors.

GAMES FOR GAMBLERS AND TEACHERS

Like many games of chance, mah-jongg and dominoes have often attracted gamblers. So has cribbage, a card game in which a decorative pegboard is used to keep score. Pegboards thousands of years old have been found, but cribbage itself is said to have been invented in England in the 1600's by Sir John Suckling. According to a writer of the time, Suckling "played at Cards rarely well, and did use to practise by himselfe a-bed." But, the account states, he was a bit of a cheat— he made his own cards and marked them, so he could read his opponents' hands.

Suckling's honesty notwithstanding, the game gained in popularity through the 1800's. Elaborate inlaid cribbage boards and tables were ordered by the upper classes. And sailors to the New World whiled away shipboard hours with the game, keeping score on cribbage boards carved by Eskimos from walrus tusks.

Lotto is another game of chance that became popular at about the same time as cribbage. It was developed from the Italian national lottery, which has been run almost without interruption since 1530. Lotto was a forerunner of bingo, and it is played in much the same way. Players receive a game card bearing numbers. Then the game organizer draws numbers at random. If the number drawn is on a player's card, it's blocked off. The player who blocks off the entire board first wins.

But not all versions of the game have been based on luck. The Japanese developed a version of lotto called *karuta*, or "one hundred poems." In this game, the organizer reads the first line of a Japanese poem, and the players must select the correct last line from their cards. And in Western countries, various educational versions were developed in the 1800's—spelling lotto, botanical lotto, historical lotto. In these games, pictures and letters were added, and they tested the players' knowledge of various subjects.

Other educational games were also popular in the past. One elaborate game, made of rare woods and ivory and dedicated to a British princess, taught the fundamentals of music. Another, the game of goose, was a spiral board game. Depending on the pictures used in the spaces, it was used to teach history, literature, or the rewards of virtuous conduct.

But whether they were used to teach, to gamble, or simply for fun, the board games of the past make one thing clear: At all times and in all places, people love to play games.

Goose, a spiral board game of the past, was educational as well as fun. It was used to teach various subjects, depending on the kinds of pictures shown in the spaces.

A Cow of a Different Color

"Easy, Belle," said Huey, patting the cow's shoulder as he brushed her neck.

"Yeah, Belle," said Dewey. "You want to look nice for the Fair tomorrow, don't you?"

"Sure, she does," put in Louie. "She's going to win a ribbon."

"Now, boys," said Grandma Duck. "Don't count your ribbons before you win them. A lot of cows have been entered in the Fair."

"But Belle is so pretty," said Huey.

"We'll see what the judge thinks," said Grandma.

The three Junior Woodchucks had spent the summer at Grandma's farm. They had brushed Belle and exercised her. They fed her the very best hay and grain. Now they were putting the finishing touches to her coat before the Fair tomorrow. If ever a cow was shiny and clean, it was Belle.

"Come on, boys," said Grandma. "Put Belle in her stall and bed her down for the night. We all have to be up early in the morning."

The boys filled Belle's stall with sweet-smelling straw, and her manger with leafy hay. Giving her a good-night pat, they followed their grandmother to the house.

They didn't see the two eyes that peeked around the silo. They didn't see the shadowy figure that crept in the barn door.

The next morning, Huey, Dewey, and Louie jumped out of bed and scrambled into their clothes. Out to the barn they went to give Belle her breakfast.

As they entered the barn, they skidded to a stop. There was Belle's stall, but there was no Belle! The stall door stood wide open.

"Did we leave the door open?" asked Huey. His brothers shook their heads.

"We've got to find her," said Louie. "You two go look in the field. I'll tell Grandma."

All four ducks searched and searched. But Belle was nowhere to be found. Huey, Dewey, and Louie were beside themselves.

"I'm sorry, boys," said Grandma. "We don't have any more time to look for her. The Fair starts in an hour, and I have to have my entries there in time for the judging. Are you coming?"

"Sure, Grandma," sighed Huey. "You need help carrying your jellies and pickles. Maybe Belle will be here when we get home."

So they all piled into Grandma Duck's old car and headed for the Duckburg County Fair.

When the jelly judge had tasted all the jellies, Grandma's apricot and raspberry took first and second prizes. And the pickle judge had given the blue ribbon to her sweet pickle relish.

"Gosh, Grandma," said Dewey, "two ribbons! What's your secret?"

"It's no secret, boys," replied Grandma. "I just love to cook. Now why don't you boys go see something of the Fair? They have a Tilt-A-Whirl and a Dragon Maze."

"Maybe later, Grandma," said Louie. "I think we'll go over and see the dairy competition. Some of the other Junior Woodchucks have entered, and we'd like to wish them luck."

"That's a fine idea," said Grandma. "I want to look at the tractors and the quilts. I'll meet you at the dairy barn later."

All around Huey, Dewey, and Louie, as they walked through the dairy barn, other children were brushing their cows' coats and fluffing their cows' tails. The boys felt sad—if Belle hadn't wandered away, they would have been brushing and fluffing, too.

"Gosh, we're sorry," said Woodchuck Alvin. "Belle had a real good chance to win."

All the other Junior Woodchucks were sympathetic, but nothing they said could cheer up Huey, Dewey, and Louie.

Suddenly there was a lot of noise from one corner of the barn. A cow was kicking and shaking her head. She pulled and pulled, until the rope that tied her snapped.

Flinging her tail high in the air, the cow came running at Huey, Dewey, and Louie. They stretched out their arms to block the aisle, and keep her from stampeding out into

the fairgrounds. But when the cow got to Huey, she stopped. "Moo!" she cried, and she gave him a big lick on the cheek.

"What on earth?!" said Dewey, taking hold of the broken lead rope. The cow looked at him, and gave him a lick, too.

"If I didn't know better," said Dewey, as the strange cow rubbed up against his arm, "I would think this cow was Belle. But her spots are all wrong."

Then Huey looked at Dewey's sleeve, where the cow had touched him. "Maybe these aren't her real spots," he said. "Come on. Let's take her back to her stall."

At the stall where the cow had been tied, they were met by a sour-faced fellow named Lonnie. They didn't know him very well, and he had never been very friendly.

"What are you doing with my cow?" he demanded.

"I think we should ask you the same thing," said Huey, picking up a red rag and dipping it in a bucket of water.

"What do you mean?" said Lonnie.

Huey rubbed at a patch of white on the cow's coat. As he rubbed, the white spot became gray, and the red rag became pink. "That's what I mean," said Huey. "I think this is our cow, not yours."

The cow looked around at Huey and nodded her head.

"She is not," blustered Lonnie.

"Prove it!" challenged Louie.

"How?" said Lonnie.

"Let's see you give her a bath," said Dewey.

Lonnie was caught. He knew that if he gave the cow a bath, all her extra spots would wash off.

"You win," he said. "She is your cow. I took her from your barn last night. I painted extra spots on her with white shoe polish, so you wouldn't recognize her."

"But why did you do it?" asked Huey. "You could have raised your own calf, just like we did."

"But I don't stand a chance against you Junior Woodchucks," protested Lonnie.

Just then, Grandma walked up. "What's going on, boys?" she asked.

When they had explained what had happened, they were surprised. They expected Grandma to be mad. Instead, she looked sad.

"How long have you lived in Duckburg, Lonnie?" she asked.

Lonnie hung his head. "About a month," he answered.

Grandma turned to the boys. "Did you ever invite Lonnie to join the Junior Woodchucks?" she asked.

"Well, no," said Dewey. "But . . ."

"But you should have," Grandma said. "It's up to you boys to welcome strangers. If you had been more friendly, this would never have happened."

It was the boys' turn to hang their heads. "I guess you're right," Louie admitted. Then he held out his hand to Lonnie. "Sorry," he said. "I bet it wasn't much fun watching all the other kids get ready for the Fair, and being left out."

"I'm sorry, too," said Lonnie, shaking Louie's hand. "I never should've taken your cow."

"Well, now that you're all agreed," said Grandma, "why don't you all give Belle a good bath and get her ready. The judging is in an hour."

Lonnie picked up a bucket and sponge. "I'll help," he offered, "if you don't mind."

"Great," said Huey.

Grandma beamed at the boys as they took Belle off to the wash rack.

"Listen, Lonnie," Huey was saying. "After the judging is over, why don't you come with us to the Super Slide?"

"Yeah," said Dewey, "and then we can all get some Pepper Bellies to eat."

"And some Krispy Kritters for dessert," Louie added. "Grandma," he called back to her. "Can we bring you some Pepper Bellies or Krispy Kritters?"

Grandma Duck laughed. "No, thanks," she answered. "I think I'll just have a cup of tea and some oatmeal cookies."

Crown of St. Edward—Britain's coronation crown.

Orb of Sweden's Eric XIV, who became king in 1560.

CROWN JEWELS

In 1671, a bold thief by the name of Colonel Blood crept into the Tower of London and stole the greatest treasure in all of England—the royal crown. The loss of the crown was not only a financial blow to the royal family, it was also a blow to its prestige. Encrusted with legends as thickly as with gems, the British crown—as well as the other crown jewels of Europe—was a symbol of wealth and power.

The "mother" of all the crowns of Europe can be traced back to the Middle Ages. This was the crown worn by Charlemagne at his coronation in 800. Charlemagne was the first ruler of the Holy Roman Empire, and his crown became its symbol. No one knows what happened to that coronation crown. But over the years, three other crowns were fashioned that became known as the Crown of Charlemagne—although none was ever worn by him. The first of the crowns that bore his name was made around 960. It was set with emeralds, amethysts, rubies, pearls, and sapphires. The Crown of Charlemagne was sought after by emperors and kings from the 900's to about 1800.

In theory, all the kings of Europe were vassals of the Holy Roman Emperor. But the empire's power gradually weakened. Kings declared themselves emperors in their realms, and they took on all the trappings of

Coronation sword of Charles X, the last king of France.

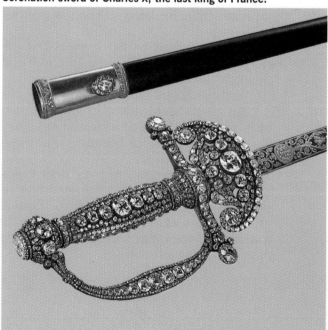

rule. In addition to crowns, they possessed other symbols of royalty. The orb was a globelike sphere carried by the ruler, to symbolize domination of the world. The scepter was a staff, symbolizing the ruler's power as a judge. And the coronation sword symbolized the ruler's military power.

Some crowns became symbols of nationalism. Hungary's Crown of St. Stephen, made about the year 1000, was one. It was honored so highly that it had its own troop of guards. At the end of World War II, it was taken to the United States. Years of negotiations brought it back to Hungary in 1978.

As their wealth and power increased, rulers amassed great collections of precious objects. In addition to crowns, orbs, scepters, and swords, these royal objects included necklaces, rings, bracelets, religious crosses, inkwells, snuff boxes—anything that could be considered "treasures of the crown." They were handed down from ruler to ruler, from generation to generation. But often rulers were forced to pawn their treasures to meet expenses. And a number of these fabulous objects were stolen. The coronation sword of Charles X of France, encrusted with over 1,500 diamonds, was stolen in modern times and has never been found.

And whatever happened to Colonel Blood? He was caught—but he wasn't executed for his bold crime. The king, Charles II, offered the daring burglar a post in his guard instead!

Crown of Charlemagne, made about A.D. 960.

Snuffbox of Frederick the Great, Prussia's most famous king.

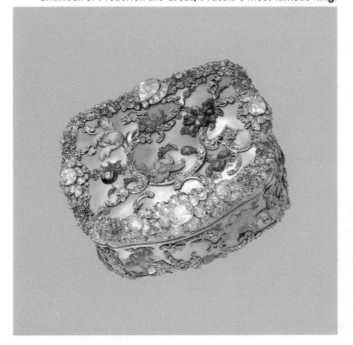

BONSAI—A LIVING ART

Japan is a land of great natural beauty—rugged mountains, rocky coasts, green hillsides, and sparkling inland seas. And the Japanese have a special art form that brings that natural beauty right into their gardens: the art of bonsai.

Bonsai (pronounced bone-sigh) are miniature plants, usually trees, that are grown in shallow containers. They have been carefully dwarfed and shaped by special techniques. The magic of bonsai is that they duplicate the appearance of full-size trees in their natural settings—perhaps a hardy pine sprouting from a mountain crevice or a stately elm towering over a plain. And they please the eye, projecting an air of tranquility and simplicity.

AN ANCIENT ART

The origins of this unique art form are shrouded in time. The Japanese name "bonsai" comes from the Chinese words *p'en tsai,* meaning "tray planted." It's thought that bonsai were first created in China 700 or 800 years ago. Many scholars think that bonsai traveled from China to Japan in the 1300's, although some say the Japanese may have taken up the art earlier.

One thing, however, is certain: The Japanese have so refined the art of growing bonsai that today this art is considered their own. Japanese gardeners may spend lifetimes working on bonsai, and they pass on their art to their children. Some Japanese bonsai are hundreds of years old. These an-

Bonsai are miniature trees that are grown in shallow containers. They began as normal trees—but then were carefully dwarfed and shaped by special techniques. Flowering trees, such as this Taiwan cherry, make especially beautiful bonsai.

cient trees, twisted and gnarled, are the work of many hands. Each gardener subtly shaped the tree and influenced its growth according to his or her own designs.

Small wonder that the graceful bonsai, which are said to symbolize mortality and the seasons, are prized in Japan—and in other countries, too. Many people in the United States and Canada enjoy creating bonsai. And the U.S. National Arboretum in Washington, D.C., includes a collection of 53 bonsai, a gift from Japan to mark the U.S. Bicentennial in 1976. The plants range from 30 to 350 years in age. One is a 180-year-old red pine that once belonged to Japan's imperial household.

HOW BONSAI ARE CREATED

Typical bonsai are 2 to 3 feet (60 to 90 centimeters) tall. They are usually developed from young plants found in nature or pur-

chased in nurseries. As the plants grow, they are pruned, pinched, and trained to dwarf and shape them.

Occasionally a bonsai is developed from a tree found in the wild that has been dwarfed by nature—especially one that has been beaten and buffeted by wind and weather so that it has already taken on an interesting shape. All that remains to be done is to refine and complete what nature has begun. Most of the very old bonsai began in this way.

The plants usually used for bonsai are hardy trees and shrubs. Evergreens such as pine and juniper are especially popular, and varieties of holly, maple, and flowering trees are often used. The best plants are those that naturally have small leaves, flowers, and fruits. Even when a tree is being grown as a miniature, it will bear full-size fruits and flowers. If they are large, the effect of the miniature will be spoiled.

Hardy trees and shrubs are usually used for bonsai. And several distinct bonsai styles have been developed. Above left: Slanting juniper. Above right: Informal upright black pine. Below: Juniper forest.

The first step in creating a bonsai is to prune the plant, to reveal the structure of the trunk and branches. At the same time, the roots are pruned sharply. From then on, new growth is pinched back regularly, as often as the growing pattern of the plant requires, to encourage compact growth. And the plant is repotted every so often, to prune the roots again and to add fresh soil.

To bend trees into interesting shapes that mimic nature, bonsai gardeners use several techniques. One is to wrap soft copper wire around the trunk and branches and then bend the parts into the desired shape. The wire is removed as the trunk or branch grows thicker. To bend a tree over, wires are attached from the tree to the rim of the pot. And weighted strings are sometimes attached to branches, to make them sweep gracefully down.

The techniques that are applied to the plant are aimed at developing the characteristics of a large, mature tree. The actual age of the bonsai is not important. What is important is that the bonsai must *look* old. For example, a good bonsai should have a trunk that is wide at the base and tapers naturally toward the top. Exposed roots help the effect, especially if they are gnarled.

Even mature bonsai require a lot of care. In Japan, most are kept outdoors, sometimes under a lathe shelter. The shelter—made of evenly spaced strips of wood—allows light to enter but protects the plants from hot sun, driving rain, and strong winds. Hardy trees such as pines and maples grow best outdoors. They need the period of dormancy that cold winter weather brings.

Fig trees and other subtropical species are sometimes grown as indoor bonsai. Indoor bonsai are especially popular in the United States. These plants grow faster than outdoor bonsai because they aren't dormant during the winter. And their naturally shallow root systems adapt well to pots.

Whatever their location, the trees are watered daily, misted often, and fed at different times depending on the species of tree. Major pruning is done in spring.

BONSAI STYLES AND SETTINGS

Over the centuries, several distinct styles of bonsai have developed. What style a gardener chooses to create depends as much on the natural growth pattern of the tree as on personal preference.

Perhaps the easiest and simplest is the informal upright style. The tree is trained to grow with a gently curving trunk and three or more branches—usually one to the left, one to the right, and one to the rear for a sense of depth.

Also popular is the slanting style, with a leaning trunk and just one or two graceful, sweeping branches. The slanting, windswept style mimics the look of weatherbeaten trees: All the branches are trained to grow on one side.

The cascade style is an extreme version of the slant—the top of the tree extends below the bottom of the container. To create a slanting or cascade effect, gardeners sometimes set the tree into the pot at an angle.

There are also multiple-trunk and "forest" bonsai. A multiple-trunk bonsai is a single tree with a trunk that divides at soil level. A forest bonsai is made up of several trees.

Trees of the same species are generally used, but two different species may also be effective. Sometimes a bonsai forest is created from a single tree. The tree is placed in a pot on its side and covered with soil, and its side branches grow up to become the miniature trees of the arrangement.

A special style is *mame* (pronounced mahmay), which means "little bean." *Mame* are miniature miniatures—bonsai less than 6 inches (15 centimeters) tall. The same techniques are used as for larger bonsai, and the same styles are created. But because of the size of the plants, there are rarely more than three branches on a *mame*.

Just as important as the shape of the tree are the container and the setting of the bonsai. Containers should be simple, in muted colors. The idea is to complement the tree, not draw attention away from it, so wood and earthenware are commonly used.

Most containers are shallow, not more than a third as tall as the tree itself. As a rule, the tree's branches should extend beyond the sides of the container. Upright, slanted, and windswept trees often look best in shallow oval or rectangular pots, especially when they are placed slightly off center. Cascade bonsai are often planted in somewhat deeper pots. The pot is then placed on a stand of some sort, so that the tree's branches can sweep down below it.

The bonsai's planting should reflect the setting that a full-size tree would have in nature. Upright and gently slanting styles are usually surrounded by level or slightly sloping soil, and the soil may be covered with a layer of soft green moss, suggesting a meadow. Small figurines can be added—perhaps a house or a tiny bridge. In Japan, these miniatures are called *bonkai*.

To suggest a rugged cliff, the roots of the plant can be exposed and trained over a rock. Such "stone-clasping" bonsai are among the most attractive. Sometimes several bonsai are grouped in the crevices of a large rock, suggesting a windswept islet.

Whatever setting is selected for a bonsai, the tree should remain the central feature. And the arrangement should have what the Japanese call *gei*, a quality of pleasing harmony. A bonsai is truly a living work of art —a bit of nature scaled down and perfected.

INDEX

ILLUSTRATION CREDITS
AND ACKNOWLEDGMENTS

14– Artist, Susan M. Waitt
17
18 David Hughes—Bruce Coleman
19 Kim Taylor—Bruce Coleman
20 ©Tim Davis—Photo Researchers
21 Courtesy IBM
22 Courtesy Viewdata Corporation of America
24 Dan Wynn
26– Artist, Michèle McLean
29
34 Dunn—DPI
35 Robert Maier—Animals Animals
37 ©D. P. Hershkowitz—Bruce Coleman
42– Maggie Steber—Jullien
43 Photo
44 Paul J. Sutton—©Duomo 1984
45 Adam J. Stoltman—©Duomo 1984
46 Focus On Sports; Adam J. Stoltman—©Duomo 1984
47 Paul J. Sutton—©Duomo 1984
48 Focus on Sports
49 Paul J. Sutton—©Duomo 1984; John Ficara—Newsweek
50– David Madison—
51 ©Duomo 1984
53 Craft by Jenny Tesar
54 Bill Ivy; Richard Brown; Bill Ivy
55 Ted Levin—Earth Scenes; John Shaw—Bruce Coleman; Brian Milne—Earth Scenes; Bill Ivy
57– Artist, Dale Barsamian
59

60 ©1984 Neil Leifer—Camera 5
61 Bart Bartholomew—©1984 Black Star
66 Margot Conte—Animals Animals
67 Francois Merlet—Bruce Coleman; Charles G. Summers, Jr.,—DPI
68 ©John-Paul Ferrero—Ardea London Ltd.
69 Gary W. Griffen—Animals Animals
70 ©Hans Pfletschinger—Peter Arnold
71 ©H. S. Terrace—Animals Animals
72– Jenny Tesar
73
74– ©Walt Disney
77 Productions
78– ©Kjell B. Sandved
79
80 Dickman—Liaison
81 Tannenbaum—Sygma
82 ©Randy Taylor—Sygma
84– Tova Navarra
85
86– Crafts by Jenny Tesar
89
95 Artist, Frank Senyk
96 Courtesy Capital Children's Museum
98 Ron Colbroth
99 Courtesy Capital Children's Museum; Ron Colbroth
100– Courtesy Ford Motor
101 Company
102– Courtesy Scholastic
105 Photography Awards, conducted by Scholastic Magazines, Inc., and sponsored by Eastman Kodak Company
106 Jeff Foott—Bruce

Coleman; Joe McDonald—Animals Animals; P. Morris—Ardea London Ltd.
107 Michael and Barbara Reed—Animals Animals; ©Owen Newman—Nature Photographers Ltd.; Joe McDonald—Bruce Coleman
109 Borromeo—Art Resource; National Museum of Ethnology, Leiden, Holland
110 Artothek—Bayer Nationalmuseum
111 Victoria and Albert Museum
116 By permission of the controller of Her Britannic Majesty's Stationery Office. ©British Crown; Artist, Karl-Erik Granath—the treasury, the royal palace, Stockholm; Cliché des Musées Nationaux
117 Christies; Kunsthistorisches Museum, Vienna
118 Courtesy Nippon Bonsai Association
120 Photo by Chuck Van de Merlen, bonsai by Phil Tacktill, Jui San Bonsai, Old Bethpage, N.Y.; Courtesy Nippon Bonsai Association; Photo by Chuck Van de Merlen, bonsai by Phil Tacktill, Jui San Bonsai, Old Bethpage, N.Y.